BHAJAN

Western Notes

Part-3

Famous Bhajans in English
and its Western Notations

Vinod Kumar

Notion Press

NOTION PRESS

India. Singapore. Malaysia.

ISBN:

Vinod Kumar

DEDICATION

This book is dedicated to my Parents.

-Vinod Kumar

CONTENTS

JAI SITA RAM

We have got this life for four days. Do not waste time. You have taken birth as human being with great fortune. Make this life beautiful by praying and worshipping God. This life is running very fast and busy but you have to spare some time for praying and worshipping Sri Hari. At the end of life nothing will go with you, only your prayers and kirtan bhajan will take you across this false world. Sing the bhajans and get the Moksh at the feet of Bhagwan Laxmi Narayana.

Siyavar Ramchandra ki Jai. Om Namah Shivaya.

-Vinod Kumar

Vinod Kumar

PREFACE

My hearty greetings and Namaste to Readers. I have written 51 Songs' Sargam books of Mukesh-1,2, Kishor-1,2, Lata, Asha, Manna dey, Yesudas, Kumar Shanu, Rafi-1,2,3,4 and SD Burman's composed song book in Hindi Language and translated many books in English SARGAM and Western CDEFG. Bhajan Swarlipi 1,2,3 and one Gazal Sargam book is also published in Hindi.

All these books are available online. Now I have translated the Bhajan book and presented as Bhajan Western Notes, Part-3 book in CDEF notes, so that devoties can play and sing bhajans and get enjoyed. A person having basic knowledge of music can play the bhajans on any instrument.

Mostly song's notations are written in original scale but somewhere you have to transpose +1 or − 1 or ±2 to get original scale. Sa taken is also mentioned in each song's detail. Person who knows western notations can understand as given below:

.नी	.नी	सा	रे॒	रे	ग॒	ग	म
.N̲	.N	S	R̲	R	G̲	G	M
.B^b	.B	C	D^b	D	E^b	E	F
.A$^\#$	.B	C	C$^\#$	D	D$^\#$	E	F

म॑	प	ध॒	ध	नी॒	नी	सां	रें॒
M*	P	D̲	D	N̲	N	S'	R̲'
G^b	G	A^b	A	B^b	B	C'	D$^{b'}$
F$^\#$	G	G$^\#$	A	A$^\#$	B	C'	C$^{\#'}$

In this book some symbols are given as (G-) it means you have to play G for two beats duration or matra similarly you have to play for the beats for more number of – if there are more dashes. When two notes are written adjacending to each other it means you have to play the notes in one beat or matra as MP mapa is played in one beat.

Lower Octave notes are written in this book by putting a dot before the note as $.G^b$ .G $.A^b$ .A $.B^b$ .B

Middle Octave notes are written normal as C D^b D E^b E F $F^\#$ G A^b A B^b B Higher Octave notes are written by putting an appostrophy on the note as C' $D^{b'}$ D' $E^{b'}$ E' F' $F^{\#'}$ G' etc.

Notations at the beginning of the song are prelude and notations in the middle of the song are interlude. These notations are written by me by my experience. Hope readers shall understand, like and enjoy it.

One has to practice sargam daily and its palte also so that one can become expert in playing difficult notes sequence. People can enjoy your playing instruments and then only your success will be counted. Care has been taken to provide accuracy still there is no liability of correctness and accuracy of notes and writer, printer, publisher and editor is not respoinsible for any error or ommissions or mistakes. If any mistake is found kindly inform.

For purchasing the books in India, one can visit notionpress.com or flipkart.com and amazon.in. Kindly review my books at amazon and flipkart and give proper stars after purchasing my books from the above sites. For any query, email to me.

- Vinod Kumar (vinod66vk@gmail.com)

Vinod Kumar

SARGAM

SARGAM swars/sound are derived from voice of animals and birds. C scale is as follows:-

Note Name	Swar	स्वर नाम	Swar full name	स्वर का पूरा नाम हिंदी में	यह स्वर किस पशु पछी की आवाज से लिया गया है.
C=	Sa=	सा	Shadaj	षडज	Peacock/ मोर की आवाज़
D=	Re=	रे	Rishabh	रिषभ	Papiha /पपीहा की आवाज़
E=	Ga=	ग	Gandhar	गन्धार	Goat/ बकरा की आवाज़
F=	Ma=	म	Madhyam	मध्यम	Crane/ बगुला की आवाज़
G=	Pa=	प	Pancham	पंचम	Koccoo/Koyal/ कोयल की आवाज़
A=	Dha=	ध	Dhaiwat	धैवत	Frog/ दादुर या मेंढक की आवाज़
B=	Ni=	नी	Nishad	निषाद	Elephant हाथी की आवाज़
C'=	Sa'=	सां	(Higher Sa)		

C#=R̲e=र̲े (रे कोमल), D#=G̲a=ग̲ (ग कोमल), F#=Ma*=मे (म तीव्र), G#=D̲ha=ध̲ (ध कोमल), A#=N̲i=न̲ी (नी कोमल)

We can write as S R̲ R G̲ G M M* P D̲ D N̲ N S'

All notes underlined are called Komal Swar as Komal Re Komal Ga Komal Dha Komal Ni. One note Ma* is called Tivra Ma Sequence of the notes are-

S	R̲	R	G̲	G	M	M*
सा	र̲े	रे	ग̲	ग	म	मे
C	D^b	D	E^b	E	F	G^b
C	$C^\#$	D	$D^\#$	E	F	$F^\#$

P	D̲	D	N̲	N	S'
प	ध̲	ध	न̲ी	नी	सां
G	A^b	A	B^b	B	C'
G	$G^\#$	A	$A^\#$	B	C'

Sa and Pa are Shudha Swar they do not have any Komal or Tivra. They are fixed notes as per North Indian music tradition.

OCTAVE

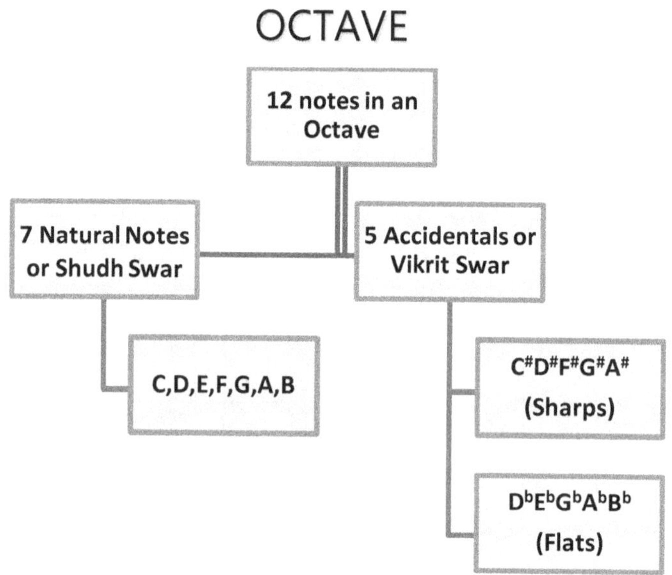

Sequence of the notes on any instrument are:

.B^b .B C D^b D E^b E F G^b G A^b A B^b B C′ D$^{b′}$ D′ so on…

.A$^#$ .B C C$^#$ D D$^#$ E F F$^#$ G G$^#$ A A$^#$ B C′ C$^{#′}$ D′ D$^{#′}$

C Scale is given as: **C D E F G A B C′**

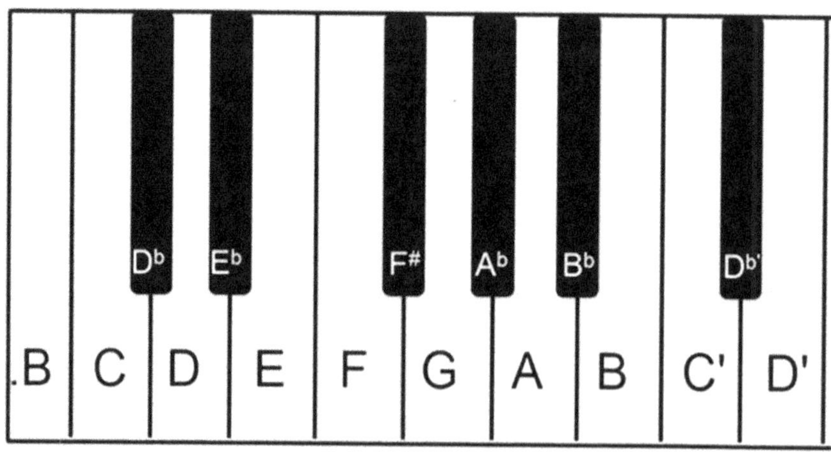

Vinod Kumar

C# Scale is given as:

$$C^{\#}\ D^{\#}\ F\ F^{\#}\ G^{\#}\ A^{\#}\ C'\ C^{\#\prime}$$

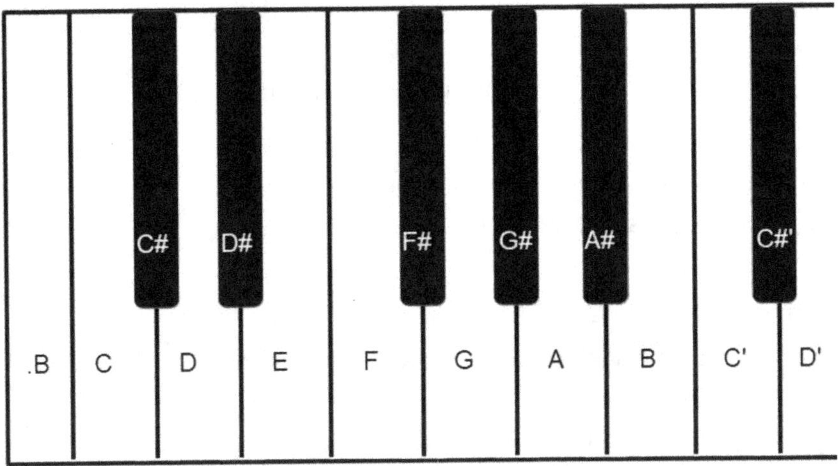

1. AE RI MAIN TO PREM DEEWANI

Film: Nau Bahaar (1952)
Lyrics: Meera bai, Shailendra
Taal: Kaharwa

Music: Raushanlal Nagrath
Singer: Lata Mangeshkar
Chord: CE^{b}G GB^{b}D' E^{b}GC'   S=C

ae ri main to prem deewaani mera dard na jaane koye -2

na main jaanu aarti vandan, naa poojaa kii riit
hai anjaani daras deewaani, merii paagal priit

li ae re maine do nainon ke, deepak liye sanjoy
ae ri main to prem deewaani, mera dard na jaane koye-2

aashaa ke phoolon ki maalaa, saanson ke sangeet
in par phooli chali rijhaane, apne man kaa meet

li ae ri maine nain dor mein, sapne liye piroye
ae ri main to prem deewaani, mera dard na jaane koye -2

Vinod Kumar

AE RI MAIN TO PREM DEEWANI

dha	ge	n	ti	n	ke	dhi	n	dha	ge	n	ti	n	ke	dhi	n
1	2	3	4	5	6	7	8	1	2	3	4	5	6	7	8

$E^{b'}$ $E^{b'}$ $D'E^{b'}$ $D'E^{b'}D'C'$ $C'E^{b'}D'C'$
na main janu aa-rti vn--d--n,

GA^{b} $GFGC'$ $C'D'E^{b'}D'$ C'
na- pu-ja- ki--- rit,

B BBC' $C'D'$ $C'D'$ $B^{b}B^{b}B^{b}$ $AGAB^{b}AG$ AGF $E^{b}CE^{b}A^{b}$ G
hai anjani------- drs diva—ni-, meri- pa-gl prit,

C' C' $D'E^{b'}$ $D'C'$ C' $C'C'D'$ AG C'-$C'D'$ $B^{b}AG$ $FE^{b}FE^{b}$
li ae ri- maine do naino- ke--, di-pk liye- snjo-y

$E^{b}F$ $GC'B^{b}$ A G GAG FFG $FE^{b}F$-E^{b}
e- ri- - main to pre-m divani, me-ra- -

$CE^{b}F$ G $FE^{b}FCE^{b}$ G
drd na ja--ne-- koy-2

GC' C' $GFGC'$ B^{b}-$C'D'$ $B^{b}C'AG$ A $B^{b}C'GAGC'$ $B^{b}A$ G
na- main ja-nu- aa-rti vn--d-n, na pu--ja---- ki- rit,

G $E^{b}FC'B^{b}C'$ $B^{b}C'B^{b}$ $GE^{b}FE^{b}$ $CE^{b}FG$ $E^{b}FE^{b}E^{b}$ C
hai anja--ni, drs divani, me-ri- pa-gl prit,

C' BC' $D'E^{b'}$ $D'C'$ C' C'-D' AG
li ae- ri- mainne do nai-no ke-,

$C'C'C'$ $B^{b}GA^{b}$ G-$FE^{b}F$-E^{b}-
di-pk liye-- sn-jo---y-

$E^{b}F$ $GC'B^{b}$ A G GAG FFG $FE^{b}F$-E^{b}
ae- ri- - main to pre-m divani, me-ra- -

$CE^\flat F$ G $FE^\flat FCE^\flat$ G
drd na ja--ne--   koy-2

 GG   FG $FE^\flat E^\flat$ $E^\flat$ DC   F-F $E^\flat F$ $CE^\flat G$
aasha ke- fu-lon ki mala, san-son ke-   sn-git

 GG $B^\flat B^\flat$ $C'E^{\flat\prime}D'C'$ $B^\flat B^\flat C'$ $B^\flat A$-G
in   pr   fu-li-   chli-   rijha-ne,

$AAB^\flat C'$ $B^\flat B^\flat$ AGA $GFGFE^\flat$
apne- mn ka-- mi----t

G C' C' $B^\flat AG$ A-A   GFG $FE^\flat FE^\flat$
li ae ri main-ne nai-n do-r me----

$CE^\flat FG$ $E^\flat FC$ $E^\flat G$-
spne--- liye- piroy

$E^\flat F$ $GC'B^\flat$ A   G GAG   FFG $FE^\flat F$-$E^\flat$
ae- ri- -   main   to pre-m divani, me-ra- -

$CE^\flat F$ G $FE^\flat FCE^\flat$ G
drd na ja--ne--   koy-2

Vinod Kumar

2. BHAJAN BINA CHAIN NA AAYE RAM

Film: Rafu Chakkar (1975)   Music: Kalyanji Anandji
Lyrics: Gulshan Bawra   Singer: Aziz Nazan, Kanchan
Taal: Kaharwa   Chord: GBD'   S=C#
Transpose +1 and play from C scale

dekh ke tu pinjare me panchhi kahe ko muskaye
hum sab hai is jag me kaidi tu ye samjh na paye
bhajan bina chain na aaye ram -2

koi na jane kab ho jaye -2 is jiwan ki sham is jiwan ki sham
bhajan bina chain na aaye ram

moh maya ki aas to pagle -2 hogi kabhi na puri
hogi kabhi na puri puri, hogi kabhi na puri
karte karte bhajan parbhu ka -2 mit jayeagi duri
mit jayeagi duri duri, mit jayeagi duri
hum bhakto ke -2 sath sath lo sab hi parbhu ka nam nam
bhajan bina chain na aaye ram -2

bhajan hai amarit ras ka pyala -2 sham sawere pina
sham sawere pina pina, sham sawere pina
isko pikar sara jiwan -2 masti me tu jina
masti me tu jina jina, masti me tu jina
bhakti kar to -2 ban jayenge apne bigade kam kam
bhajan bina chain na aaye ram -2

bolo ram ram ram radhe sham sham sham
sita ram ram ram radhe sham sham sham

BHAJAN BINA CHAIN NA AAYE RAM

dha	-	na	ti	na	-	dha	ti	dha	-	na	ti	na	-	dha	ti
1	2	3	4	5	6	7	8	1	2	3	4	5	6	7	8

prelude: flute: F'E'D'G'---- F'E'C' ---- D' --- C'BA --- AG

BBB   BC'--- C'D'B BC'C'   C' B-GF   G
bhjn   bina--------   chai----n na aa-ye- ram

FG   B BB C'B AG GGAF
koii n jane kb ho- jaye--

FG   B BB C'B AG GG
koii n jane kb ho- jaye

BB D'E'E'F' E'D' D' ---- D'E'E'D'—B
is ji-vn   ki- sham

BB D'E'E'F' E'D' D' --
is ji-vn   ki- sham

BBB BC'--- C'D'B BC'C'   C' B-GF   G
bhjn bina--------   chai----n na aa-ye- ram

interlude:

D F G ---- A B B G --- F D
D F G ---- A B B G --- F D
E' E' E' E' D' E' D' C C' C' D' C' B A B A G
E' E' E' E' D' E' D' C C' C' D' C' BC'-B AB-AG-
D FG – AB-A G—FFG--

Vinod Kumar

F   GBB   B C'BA G GGAF
moh ma-ya ki aa-s to pgle-

F   GBB   B C'BA G GGG
moh ma-ya ki aa-s to pgle

BD' E'E'F'-   E'D' D'D'---- D'E'E'--D'—B-
hogi kbhi--   na- puri

BD' E'E'F'-   E'D' D'D' G' – F'E'D'B
hogi kbhi--   na- puri, pu-ri----

BD' E'E'F'-   E'D' D'D'
hogi kbhi--   na- puri

FFGB BBB   C'BA GG   GAF
krte- krte   bhjn prbhu ka--

FFGB BBB   C'BA GG   G
krte- krte   bhjn prbhu ka-

BB   D'E'E'F'--E'D' D'D'
mit ja-e---   gi- duri

BB   D'E'E'F'--E'D' D'D' G' – F'E'D'B
mit ja-e---   gi- duri, du-ri-----

BB   D'E'E'F'--E'D' D'D'
mit ja-e---gi-   duri

E'D'D'E'F'A'G' D'   F'G'   G'---- F'F'G'D'
ho-------   hm   bhkton   ke

 D'   F'F'G'   G'   F'F'   F'E'E'   D'
hm bhkton ke   sath   sa-th   lo,

D'E'   E'   E'D'E'D'E'   D'C'   C'   D'E'D'C'BAG
sb   hi   prbhu---   ka- nam, na--------m

BBB   BC'--- C'D'B   BC'C'   C' B-GF   G
bhjn   bina--------   chai----n na aa-ye- ram,

FFG   B   BBB   C'B AG   G-GA-F
bhjn hai amrit   rs   ka- pyala---,

FFG   B   BBB   C'B AG   GG
bhjn hai amrit   rs   ka- pyala,

BD'   E'E'F'--E'D'   D'D' -----D'E'E'-D'- B
sham sve----re--   pina

BD'   E'E'F'--E'D'   D'D'   G' – F'E'D'B
sham sve----re--   pina pina

BD'   E'E'F'--E'D'   D'D'
sham sve----re--   pina

FFGB   B B C'BAG G-GAG
isko-   pi kr sa-ra- jivn--,

Vinod Kumar

FFGB   B B C'BAG GG
isko-   pi kr sa-ra- jivn,

BBD'E' E'F'   E'D' D'D' D'E'E'-D'—B-
msti-   me- tu- jina-----,

BBD'E' E'F'   E'D' D'D'   G' – F'E'D'B
msti-   me- tu- jina,   ji-na-----

BBD'E' E'F' E'D' D'D'
msti-   me- tu- jina

E'D'D'E'F'A'G' D'D'F' G'G' G'---- F'F'E'D'
o--------   bhkti   kr   to--------

D'D'F' G'G' G' G'F' F'E'D'
bhkti   kr   to bn jayenge

D'E'E' D'E'D'C' C'---- D'E'D'C'BAG--
apne   bigde- kam, ka--------m

BBB   BC'--- C'D'B BC'C'   C' B-GF   G
bhjn   bina-------- chai----n na aa-ye- ram,

GA   C'   C'   C' BA   F   F   F
bolo ram ram ram radhe shyam shyam shyam

GA   B   B   B AF   G   G   G
sita ram ram ram radhe shyam shyam shyam

3. CHALO BULAWA AAYA HAI

Film: Avtar (1983)   Music: Laxmikant Pyarelal
Lyrics: Anand Bakshi   Singer: Chanchal, Mahendra Kapoor, Asha
Taal: Kaharwa   Chord: CE^bG S=A (very high scale)
                Transpose +9 and play from C scale

(You can play in low scale according to your convenience)

maata jinko yaad kare woh log nirale hote hai

maata jinka naam pukare kismat wale hote hai

chalo bulawa aaya hai maata ne bulaya hai -3

jai maata di

chalo bulawa aaya hain maata ne bulaya hain

ho unnchhe parvat pe raani maa ne darbaar lagaya hai

chalo bulawa aaya hain maata ne bulaya hain

jai maata di

chalo bulawa aaya hain maata ne bulaya hain

saare jag mein ek thikana saare gam ke maaro ka

saare jag mein ek thikana saare gam ke maaro ka

ho, rastaa dekh rahi hai maata apani aankh ke taaron ka

rastaa dekh rahi hai maata apani aankh ke taaron ka

ho, mast hawaon ka ek jhonka yeh sandesaa laaya hai

chalo bulawa aaya hain maata ne bulaya hain

jai maata di

jai maata di jai maata di, kehte jaaon, jai maata di

jai maata di jai maata di, kehte jaaon jai maata di

jai maata di kehte jaao aane jaane walon ko

chalte jaaon tum mat dekho apne paaon ke chhalon ko

chalte jaaon tum mat dekho apne paaon ke chhalon ko

ho, jisne jitna dard saha hai utna chain bhi paaya hai

Vinod Kumar

chalo bulawa aaya hai maata ne bulaya hai, jai maata di

vaishno devi ke mandir mein -2 log muraaden paate hai
o rote rote aate hain hanste hanste jaate hain
o rote rote aate hain hanste hanste jaate hain
ho, main bhi maang ke dekhu jisne jo maanga woh paaya hain
chalo bulawa aaya hai maata ne bulaya hai
jai maata di

main bhi toh ek maa hu maata, maa hi maa ko pehchane -2
bete ka dukh kya hota hai aur koi yeh kya jaane
ho, uska khoon main dekhu kaise jisko dudh pilaya hain
ho chalo bulawa aaya hai maata ne bulaya hai
ho chalo bulawa aaya hai maata ne bulaya hai

chalo bulawa aaya hai maata ne bulaya hai
chalo bulawa aaya hai maata ne bulaya hai
toh prem se bolo- jai maata di
saare bolo-jai maata di
jai maata di jai maata di
vaishno raani -jai maata di
ambe kalyani-jai maata di
maa bholi bhali-jai maata di
maa shero wali-jai maata di
jholi bhar deti-jai maata di
sankat har leti-jai maata di
o jai maata di jai maata di
jai maata di -4.

CHALO BULAWA AAYA HAI

dhage	nati	nke	dhin	dhage	nati	nke	dhin	dhage	nati	nke	dhin	dhage	nati	nke	dhin
12	34	56	78	12	34	56	78	12	34	56	78	12	34	56	78

GG   GB^b B^{b}A^{b}B^{b}A^b GG G GF FFFE^b E^{b}FGF   F—GE^b

mata jinko ya--d   kre vo log nirale ho---te hain-----

GG   GA^{b}G-E^b E^{b}FGF FFF—E^{b}D^{b}C.B^b .B^{b}CCC CE^{b}E^b E^{b}D^b C

mata jinka-   na---m pukare -------- kismt va-le hote hain

prelude:

CE^b-F-A^b- E^{b}A^{b}GFE^b C.B^b.A^b-

.A^b.B^{b}CE^b-D- C.B^{b}D^{b}CC

.B^b.B^b .B^{b}CD^b CC D^b.B^b .B^b.B^b C   D^{b}CC   C

chlo   bulava aaya hai mata ne bulaya hai -2

A^b—GF E^{b}D^{b}C

o-------

.B^{b}C CCD^{b}E^{b}D^{b}C CD^{b}E^b E^b-D^{b}C .B^b.B^b C CCD^b-E^{b}D^b C   C

chlo bula----va- aa-ya hai--   mata ne bula—---ya- hai

G GG   G

jy mata di

FE^{b}CD^{b}F FF E^{b}D^{b}CD^b E^b FF   FE^{b}A^b A^b A^{b}GF-E^b D^{b}FF E^{b}D^{b}C.B^b

o------ uche prbt pe rani ma-- ne drba-r lgaya hai------

.B^{b}C CCD^{b}E^{b}D^{b}C CD^{b}E^b E^b-D^{b}C .B^b.B^b C CCD^{b}E^{b}D^b C

chlo bula----va- aa-ya hai--   mata ne bula—ya- hai

Vinod Kumar

A♭   A♭A♭   A♭
jy   mata   di

.B♭C   CCD♭E♭D♭C   CD♭E♭   E♭-D♭C   .B♭.B♭   C   CCD♭E♭D♭   C
chlo   bula----va-   aa-ya   hai-----   mata   ne   bula—ya-   hai

interlude:
GA♭GFE♭D♭E♭FCD♭E♭
CD♭ E♭- F- CD♭ F#-F- -2
CD♭E♭ CD♭E♭ CD♭E♭ FG—

GG   FF   E♭   FG GG-FE♭   FF E♭D♭   F   E♭D♭   C
sare jg   me ek thikana sare gm ke maron ka

.B♭.B♭   .B♭ C   D♭   CCC   C.B♭   .B♭ C   D♭C   C
sare   jg me ek thikana sare   gam ke maron ka

G-FE♭   GG   FE♭   E♭F G   GFE♭   FF   E♭D♭F   F   E♭D♭ C
o---   rasta dekh rhi hai mata apni aankh ke taron ka

.B♭.B♭   .B♭   CD♭ C   CC   C.B♭   .B♭   C   D♭C C
rasta   dekh rhi hai mata   apni aankh ke taron ka

FE♭CD♭F FF   FE♭-CD♭   E♭ FF   FFE♭A♭   A♭ A♭FE♭D♭   FF   E♭-D♭C
o-----   mst hva-on- ka ek jhonka- ye sndesa- laya hai----

.B♭C   CCD♭E♭D♭C   CD♭E♭   E♭-D♭C   .B♭.B♭ C   CCD♭E♭D♭   C
chlo   bula----va-   aa-ya hai-----   mata ne   bula—ya- hai

 G   GG   G
jy   mata di

.B♭ CD♭   C E♭   E♭D♭ C   E♭E♭   D♭C E♭ E♭D♭   C
jy mata   di jy mata di... khte jao jy mata di

.B♭ CD♭   C E♭   E♭D♭ C   .B♭C   D♭C   E♭   E♭D♭   C
jy mata di jy mata di... khte jao   jy mata   di

G   GG   G   GA♭ GG   GA♭   GF   E♭F   FE♭
jy mata di. khte jao aane jane valon ko-

 GG   FE♭   E♭   FE♭   D♭C   .B♭C   D♭   C   CC   C
chlte jao tum mt dekho apne panv ke chhalon ko -2

FE♭CD♭F   FFF   E♭D♭CD♭ E♭F   FF   FE♭A♭
 ho----- jisne jitna   drd saha hai---

A♭A♭A♭   FE♭   D♭   FF   E♭E♭D♭C
utna chain bhi paya   hai-----

.B♭C   CCD♭E♭D♭C   CD♭E♭ E♭-D♭C .B♭.B♭   C   CCD♭E♭E♭D♭ C
chlo bula----va- aa-ya hai--   mata   ne bula—-ya- hai

 G   GG   G
jy mata di
interlude:
F---- FGFE♭G---- FGFE♭F—
B♭ G- F- E♭FE♭D♭E♭ –
C D♭ F F F E♭ E♭ E♭ E♭ D♭ E♭ D♭ C- -2 C G –

 GG   GG GF A♭FE♭   E♭   GA♭ GA♭-FE♭   E♭FGF   F
vaishno devi ke- mandir me, log muraden - pa-te- hain

Vinod Kumar

F   FE♭ FD♭ CC   F   FF   E♭D♭   CC   C
o   rote rote aate   hain, hnste hnste jate hain

.B♭C   D♭C CC   E♭   E♭E♭   E♭D♭   CC   C
rote   rote aate   hain, hnste hnste   jate   hain

FE♭CD♭F   F   F   E♭C   D♭   E♭F   FFFE♭A♭
ho------ main bhi mang ke dekhu jisne—

A♭   A♭F   E♭D♭   FF   E♭E♭D♭C
jo manga vo- paya hai-----

.B♭C CCD♭E♭D♭C CD♭E♭ E♭-D♭C .B♭.B♭   C CCD♭E♭D♭   C
chlo bula----va- aa-ya hai----- mata   ne bula—ya- hai

 G   GG   G
jy mata di

interlude:
F—GA♭GFE♭FG - GA♭GFE♭FG –
E♭FGFE♭GF—E♭FGFE♭FGA♭B♭-
C'—B♭A♭GFE♭ --- FE♭ A♭— GFE♭D♭-
C D♭ E♭ F G F E♭ D♭ .B♭.B♭ C .B♭.B♭ C
C D♭ E♭ F G F E♭ D♭ .B♭.B♭ C FE♭D♭E♭C

FE♭   FG   GF FE♭ E♭D♭   F   E♭D♭C
main- bhi- to- ek ma- hun ma-ta,

E♭   E♭ FG G   FE♭GFF
ma hi ma- ko phcha-ne

FE♭FG GF   FE♭   E♭D♭ FE♭D♭   C   E♭E♭   E♭FG G   FE♭   GFF
be-te- ka- dukh kya hota- hai aur   koii- ye kya ja-ne

_E♭CF FFF   E♭C   D♭   E♭F   FFE♭A♭
o---- uska   khun main dekhu kaise--

A♭A♭A♭   FE♭   D♭FF   E♭E♭D♭C
jisko   dudh pilaya   hai-----

.B♭C   CCD♭E♭D♭C CD♭E♭ E♭-D♭C .B♭.B♭ C CCD♭E♭D♭   C
chlo bula----va- aa-ya hai--- mata ne bula—ya- hai

.B♭.B♭   .B♭CD♭ CC   D♭.B♭   .B♭.B♭ C D♭CC   C
chlo   bulava aaya hai- mata ne bulaya hai -2

E♭   E♭E♭   E♭DC CC   E♭   .B♭.B♭ C   D♭CC   C
o chlo bulava aaya hai mata   ne bulaya hai -2

B♭C′ C′D♭′C′B♭G-E♭- FGA♭G F-E♭D♭ CE♭   E♭—D♭   D♭FD♭ C
chlo bula-va----   aa-ya- hai---- mata ne--- bulaya hai -2

E♭   E♭   E♭ D♭C .B♭ CD♭ C
to prem se bolo- jy mata di

E♭   D♭E♭   D♭C .B♭ CD♭ C
o   sare bolo- jy mata di...

E♭   D♭   E♭ D♭ C .B♭ CD♭ C
o   jy   mata di jy mata di

Vinod Kumar

D♭E♭E♭   D♭C .B♭ CD♭   C
vaishno rani-jy mata di

E♭D   E♭D♭C .B♭ CD♭ C
ambe klyani- jy mata di

D♭   .B♭D♭ CC .B♭ CD♭   C
man bholi bhali-jy mata di

D♭ .B♭D♭   CC.B♭ CD♭   C
ma shero vali-jy mata di

E♭ D   E♭ D♭C .B♭ CD♭ C
jholi bhr deti- jy mata di

E♭ D E♭   D♭C .B♭ CD♭ C
snkt hr   leti-jy mata di

D♭ .B♭ D♭ C   C .B♭ CD♭ C
o jy ma ta   di... jy mata di

G GA♭B♭A♭C′   C′
jy ma- ---ta   di

D♭′   D♭′D♭′   C′D♭′
jy   ma ta   di-

C′---D♭′E♭′   D♭′E♭′ D♭′S̲′ C′
jy-----   ma- ta- di
.B♭ CD♭   C
jy ma ta   di x 16

4. DUNIYA BANANE WALE

Film: Teesari Qasam (1966)   Music: Shanker Jaikishan
Lyrics: Hasrat Jaipuri   Singer: Mukesh
Taal: Kaharwa   Chord: EGB   S=F
Transpose +5 and play from C scale

duniya banane wale kya tere man me samayi

kahe ko duniya banayi tune kahe ko duniya banayi

kahe banaye tune maati ke putale,

dharti ye pyari pyari mukhde ye ujle

kahe banaya tune duniya ka khela -2

jisme lagaya jawani ka mela

gupchup tamasha dekhe, wah re teri khudaai

kahe ko duniya banaai tune, kahe ko duniya banaai

duniya banane wale...

tu bhi to tadpa hoga man ko bana kar

toofaan ye pyar ka man mein chhupa kar

koi chhawi to ankho mein teri -2

aansu bhi chhalke honge palko se teri

bol kya soojhi tujhko kahe ko preet jagai

kahe ko duniya banayi tune, kahe ko duniya banayi

duniya banane wale ...

preet bana k tune jeena sikhaya,

hasna sikhaya, rona sikhaya

jeevan ke path par meet milaye -2

meet mila k tune sapne jagae

sapne jaga k tune kahe ko de di judaai

kahe ko duniya banayi tune, kahe ko duniya banayi

duniya banane wale ...

Vinod Kumar

DUNIYA BANANE WALE

dhage 12	nati 34	nke 56	dhin 78	dhage 12	nati 34	nke 56	dhin 78	dhage 12	nati 34	nke 56	dhin 78	dhage 12	nati 34	nke 56	dhin 78
.A	.B	C	D	E	D	-	CD	E	D	C	.B	.A	.A	.B	-
A	G	F#	E	D	D	E	-	F#	E	D	C	.A	.A	.B	-
-	.B	.B	C	D	D	E	E	-	E	E	E	E	E	F#	E
-	duni	ya	b	na	ne	va	le	-	kya	te	re	m	n	me	s
D	E	F#	E	D	-	C	.B	-	.B	.B	C	D	D	E	C
ma	-	-	-	yi	-	-	-	-	ka	he	ko	du	ni	ya	b
.B	C	D	C	.B	-	.A	.G	-	.G	.B	C	D	D	E	C
na	-	-	-	yi	-	tu	ne	-	ka	he	ko	du	ni	ya	b
.B	C	D	C	.B	-	-	-								
na	-	-	-	yi	-	-	-								
E	F#	G	A	B	AC'	B	-	D	E	F#	G	A	GB	A	-
A	G	F#	E	D	E	-	-	.B	C	D	E	C	.B	-	-
.B	.AC	.B	-	.B	.AC	.B	-	.B	.AC	.B	.AC	.B	.AC	.B	-
-	F#	A	G	F#	F#	F#	F#	-	E	F#D	E	F#	F#	F#	-
-	ka	he	b	na	ye	tu	ne	-	ma	-ti	ke	pu	t	le	-
-	F#	A	G	F#	F#	F#	F#	-	EF#	-D	E	F#	F#	F#	-
-	dhr	ti	ye	pya	ri	pya	ri	-	mukh	-de	-ye	u	j	le	-
-	E	E	E	E	E	E	E	ED	-F#	-	E	D	C	.B	-
-	ka	he	b	na	ya	tu	ne	duni	-ya	-	ka	khe	-	la	-
-	.B	G	F#	E	-D	-	D	C	-E	-	D	C	-	.B	-
-	jis	me	l	ga	-ya	-	j	va	-ni	-	ka	me	-	la	-

-	.B	.B	C	D	D	E	E	-	C	E	E	E	-	F#	E
-	gup	chup	t	ma	sha	de	khe	-	va	h	re	te	-	ri	khu
D	E	F#	E	D	-	C	.B	-	.B	.B	C	D	D	E	C
da	-	-	-	yi	-	-	-	-	ka	he	ko	du	ni	ya	b
.B	C	D	C	.B	-	.A	.G	-	.G	.B	C	D	D	E	C
na	-	-	-	yi	-	tu	ne	-	ka	he	ko	du	ni	ya	b
.B	C	D	C	.B	-	-	-								
na	-	-	-	yi	-	-	-								

5. DUNIYA SE JANE WALE

Film: Pushpanjali (1970)
Lyrics: Anand Bakshi
Taal: Kaharwa
Transpose +1 and play from C scale

Music: Laxmikant Pyarelal
Singer: Mukesh
Chord: DGB   S=C#

jaane chale jate hai kaha

duniya se jaane wale, jaane chale jate hai kaha

kaise dhundhe koi unko, nahi kadamo ke bhi nisha

jaane hai wo

jaane hai wo kaun nagariya, aaye jaaye khat na khabariya

aaye jab jab unki yade, aaye hotho pe fariyade

jaake phir na ane wale, jaane chale jate hai kaha

duniya se jaane wale, jaane chale jate hai kaha

mere bichhade

mere bichhade jivan sathi, sathi jaise dipak bati

mujhase bichhad gaye tum aise, saawan ke jate hi jaise

ud ke badal kaale kaale, jaane chale jate hai kaha

duniya se jaane wale, jaane chale jate hai kaha

Vinod Kumar

DUNIYA SE JANE WALE

dha	ge	na	ti	na	ke	dhin	na	dha	ge	na	ti	na	ke	dhin	na
1	2	3	4	5	6	7	8	1	2	3	4	5	6	7	8
G	A	G	F#	-	G	A	A	B	B	G	-	-	-	-	GA
															duni
A	B	B	B	C'	-	B	A	G	A	G	F#	G	A	A	B
ya	se	ja	ne	va	-	le	-	ja	ne	ch	le	ja	te	hain	k
B	G	G	A	A	B	B	B	C'	-	B	A	G	A	G	F#
ha	-	du	ni	ya	se	ja	ne	va	-	le	-	ja	ne	ch	le
G	A	A	B	B	G	-G	-A	A	B	B	D'	Db'D'	-	B	A
ja	te	hain	k	ha	-	-kai	-se	dhundhe	ko	ii		un	-	ko	-
G	A	G	F#	G	A	A	B	B	G	-					
n	hi	k	d	mo	ke	bhi	ni	sha	-	-					
											B	-	-	A	G
B	-	-	C'	-	C'B	C'B	C'D'	B	-	-	F'	-	D'	-	C'B
B	-	-	C'	-	C'B	C'B	C'D'	B	-	G	AB	G	-		
														B	B
														ja	ne
C'	-	D'	-	-	-	-	-	-	-	-	C'D'	B	-	B	B
hai	-	vo	-	-	--	-	-	-	-	-	-	-	-	ja	ne
C'	-	D'	-	-	D'E'	-D'	-C'	B	C'	B	A	-	-	C'	B
hai	-	vo	-	-	kau-	-n	-n	g	ri	ya	-	-	-	aa	ye

C′	-	D′	-	-	D′E′	-D′	-C′	B	C′	B	A	-	-	B	A
ja	-	ye	-	-	kht	-n	-kh	b	ri	ya	-	-	-	aa	ye
G	G	G	G	G	G	B	A	G	G	G	G	G	G	G	A
jb	jb	un	ki	ya	den	aa	yen	ho	to	pe	fri	ya	den	ja	ke
A	B	B	D′	D♭′D′	-	B	A	G	A	G	F#	G	A	A	B
fir	na	aa	ne	va-	-	le	-	ja	ne	ch	le	ja	te	he	k
B	G	G	A	A	B	B	B	C′	-	B	A	G	A	G	F#
ha	-	du	ni	ya	se	ja	ne	va	-	le	-	ja	ne	ch	le
G	A	A	B	B	G	-G	-A	A	B	B	D′	D♭′D′	-	B	A
ja	te	hain	k	ha	-	-kai	-se	dhundhe	ko	ii	un	-	ko	-	
G	A	G	F#	G	A	A	B	B	G	-					
n	hi	k	d	mo	ke	bhi	ni	sha	-	-					

Vinod Kumar

6. GAAIYE GANPATI JAGVANDAN

Ganpati Bhajan
Lyrics: Tulasidas (Vinay Patrika)
Taal: Bhajani Theka
Raag: Maarwa Based
Transpose +1 and play from C scale

Music: Md. Husain
Singer: Ahmad Husain, Md. Husain
Chord: $D^bF^\#A$ S=C#

gaaiye ganpati jagvandan
shankar suvan bhavani ke nandan
gaaiye ganpati jagvandan

modak priya mud mangal data
vidya varidhi buddhi vidhata
gaaiye ganpati jagvandan

shiddhi sadan gaj vadan vinayak
kripa sindhu sundar sab layak
gaaiye ganpati jagvandan

maangat tulsi das kar jore
basahun ram siya manas more
gaaiye ganpati jagvandan

GAAIYE GANPATI JAGVANDAN

dhin- ndhin -dhin nn	dhin- ntin -tin nn	dhin-ndhin-dhin nn	dhin- ntin -tin nn
1 2 3 4	5 6 7 8	1 2 3 4	5 6 7 8

A-F#EDb   C.ADbDb   DbEDb-CC
ga-iye-   gnpti   jgvn-dn

EE   F#AE   EF#AF#   A   EDbCC
shnkr suvn   bhvani   ke   nn-dn

A-F#EDb   C.ADbDb   DbEDb-CC
ga-iye-   gnpti   jgvn-dn

EEE   F#AE   AA   C'C'C'   BDb'C'
modk   priy-   mud   mangl   da-ta

C'C'   BDb'BA   AF#   EF#BAA   AF#   E Db-C
vidya va-ridhi buddhi vidha--ta buddhi vidha--ta

DbCDbA-F#EDb   C.ADbDb   DbEDbCC
ga-----iye-   gnpti   jgvn-dn

A-F#EDb   C.ADbDb   DbEDb-CC
ga-iye-   gnpti   jgvn-dn

EE   EF#A   F#EC'C'C'   C'BDb'C'C'
siddhi sdn   gjvdn   vina-yk

C'C'   BDb'A   AF#A F#E F#BAA   AF#F#   EE Db-CC
kripa sindhu- sundr sb la-yk   sundr sb la-yk

_DbCDbA-F#EDb   C.ADbDb   DbEDbCC
ga-----iye-   gnpti   jgvndn

Vinod Kumar

A-F#EDᵇ C.ADᵇDᵇ DᵇEDᵇCC
ga-iye- gnpti jgvn-dn

EEE   F#AF#AC′C′   C′C′ BDᵇ′C′
mangt tulsi-das   kr jore

C′C′C′   BDᵇ′Dᵇ′AA AF#E F#BA   AF#E   Dᵇ-C
bshun   ra-m,siy mans mo-re mans mo-re

DᵇCDᵇA-F#EDᵇ C.ADᵇDᵇ DᵇEDᵇCC
ga-----iye-   gnpti   jgvndn

A-F#EDᵇ   C.ADᵇDᵇ DᵇEDᵇCC
ga-iye-   gnpti   jgvn-dn

A-F#EDᵇ   C.ADᵇDᵇ C.ADᵇDᵇ C.ADᵇDᵇ DᵇEDᵇ-CC
ga-iye-   gnpti gnpti   gnpti   jgvn-dn

7. INSAF KA MANDIR HAI YE

Film: Amar (1954)   Music: Naushad Ali
Lyrics: Shakeel Badayuni   Singer: Md. Rafi
Taal: Daadra   Chord: EGB S=C

insaaf ka mandir hai ye bhagavaan ka ghar hai
kahnaa hai jo kah de tujhe kis baat ka dar hai

hai khot tere man me jo bhagavaan se hai dur
hai paanv tere -2 phir bhi tu aane se hai majabur-2
himmat hai to aa jaa ye bhalaai ki dagar hai
insaaf ka mandir hai ye bhagavaan ka ghar hai

dukh de ke jo dukhiyo se na insaaf karegaa
bhagavaan bhi usako na kabhi maaf karegaa
ye soch le -3 har baat ki daataa ko khabar hai-2
himmat hai to aajaa ye bhalaai ki dagar hai
insaaf kaa mandir hai ye bhagavaan ka ghar hai.

hai paas tere jiski amaanat use de de
nirdhan bhi hain insaan mohobbat use de de
jis dar pe sabhi ek hain bande, ye vo dar hai
himmat hai to aajaa ye bhalaai ki dagar hai
insaaf kaa mandir hai ye bhagavaan ka ghar hai.

maayus na ho har ke taqdeer ki bazi
pyara hai vo gam jisme ho bhagawaan bhi razi
dukh dard mile -2 jisme vahi pyar amar hai
ye soch le har baat ki data ko khabar hai
insaaf kaa mandir hai...

Vinod Kumar

INSAF KA MANDIR HAI YE

dhi	na	ti	na	dhi	na	dhi	na	ti	na	dhi	na
1	2	3	4	5	6	1	2	3	4	5	6
										E	-
										in	-
E	B	B	B	B	-	B	C'	A	B	F#	F#
sa	-	f	ka	man	-	di	r	hai	ye	bh	g
F#	-	G	A	F	G	E	-	-	-	E	-
va	-	n	ka	gh	r	hai	-	-	-	in	-
E	B	B	B	B	-	C'	B	A	G	E	G
sa	-	f	ka	man	-	di	r	hai	ye	bh	g
GB	AB	A	G	E	F	E	-	-	-	E	E
va	-	n	ka	gh	r	hai	-	-	-	k	h
E	G	G	A	A	A	G	A	G	E	E	G
na	-	hai	jo	k	h	de	-	tu	jhe	ki	s
GB	AB	A	G	E	F	E	-	-	-		
ba-	--	t	ka	d	r	hai	-	-	-		
										B	-
										hai	-
G	-	A	C'	D'	-	D'	E'	E'	E'	E'	E'
kho	-	t	te	re	-	m	n	me	jo	bh	g
E'	-	E'	E'	D'	E'	C'	-	B	B	D'	-
va	-	n	se	-	hai	du	-	-	r	hai	-
E'	G'	G'	F#'	G'	-	-	-	-	-	E'	F'
paa	-	v	te	re	-	-	-	-	-	hai	-

G'	-	F'	E'	E'	-	D'	E'	E'	E'	E'	-
paa	-	v	te	re	-	fi	r	bhi	tu	aa	-
D'	F#'	E'	D'	C'	D'	D'	E'	-	-	B	C'
ne	-	se	hai	m	j	bu	-	-	r	aa	-
C'	B	A	G	G	A	F	E	-	-	E	-
ne	-	se	hai	m	j	bu	-	-	r	hi	m
E	G	G	G	G	-	G	A	A	A	A	-
m	t	hai	to	aa	-	ja	-	ye	bh	la	-
A	C'	C'	C'	C'	D'	D'	B	-	-		
ii	-	ki	d	g	r	hai	-	-	-		
										E	E
										du	kh
E	G	G	G	G	G	G	A	A	A	A	A
de	-	ke	jo	du	ni	ya	-	se	n	in	-
A	-	G	G	AB	AG	F	E	-	-	E	E
sa	-	f	k	re	-	ga	-	-	-	bh	g
E	B	B	B	B	B	A	B	A	G	A	-
va	-	n	bhi	u	s	ko	-	n	k	bhi	-
E	-	F	G	F	-	E	-	-	-	E'	-
ma	-	f	k	re	-	ga	-	-	-	ye	-
E'	G'	F#'	G'	-	-	-	-	-	-	-	-
so	-	ch	le	-	-	-	-	-	-	-	-
-	-	-	-	E'	F'	G'	-	F'	E'	-	-
-	-	-	-	ye	-	so	-	ch	le	-	-

Vinod Kumar

-	-	-	-	E'	F'	G'	-	F'	E'	E'	E'
-	-	-	-	ye	-	so	-	ch	le	h	r
D'	E'	E'	E'	E'	D'	D'E'	F#'	E'	D'	C'	D'
ba	-	t	ki	da	-	ta	-	ko	kh	b	r
D'	E'	-	-	B	C'	C'	B	A	G	G	A
hai	-	-	-	da	-	ta	-	ko	kh	b	r
F	E	-	-	E	-	E	G	G	G	G	-
hai	-	-	-	hi	m	m	t	hai	to	aa	-
G	A	A	A	A	-	A	C'	C'	C'	C'	D'
ja	-	ye	bh	la	-	ii	-	ki	d	g	r
D'	B	-	-								
hai	-	-	-								
										E	-
										in	-
E	B	B	B	B	-	B	C'	A	B	F#	F#
sa	-	f	ka	man	-	di	r	hai	ye	bh	g
F#	-	G	A	F	G	E	-	-	-	-	
va	-	n	ka	gh	r	hai	-	-	-	-	

8. KAILASH KE NIWASI NAMO BAR BAR

Shiv Bhajan

Taal: Daadra

Transpose +1 and play from C scale

Singer: Master Rana

Chord: CE^{b}G   S=C#

https://www.youtube.com/watch?v=GGpZ7fFqifk

ek bel patram ek pushpam ek lota jal ki dhaar

dayaa lorij ke dete hain chandra moli fal chaar

byaghambaram bhasmambaram jata jutli panch

aasan jamaaye baithe hain kripa singhu kailash

kailash ke niwasi, namo bar bar hu-2

aayo sharan tihari, bhole taar taar tu-2

bhakto ko kabhi shiv tune nirash na kiya

manga jinhe jo chaha vardan de diya

bada hi tera dayeja ho... bada datar tu

bada hi tera dayeja bada datar tu bada datar tu

aayo sharan tihari, bhole taar taar tu

kailash ke niwasi, namo bar bar hu

aayo sharan tihari, bhole taar taar tu

bakhaan kya karu mai rakho ke dher ka

chutki bhabhoot me hai khajana kuber ka

he ganga dhar mukti dwar ho....

He ganga dhar mukti dwar om kaar tu, prabhu om kaar tu

aayo sharan tihari, bhole taar taar tu-2

kailash ke niwasi, namo bar bar hu

aayo sharan tihari, bhole taar taar tum

hey gang dwar mukti dwar om kaar tu

gang dwar mukti dwar om kaar tu

aayo sharan tihari, bhole taar taar tu

Vinod Kumar

kailash ke niwasi, namo bar bar hu
aayo sharan tihari, bhole taar taar tu

kya kya nahi diya hai, hum kya pramaan de
base gaye hain trilok shambo tere daan se
zahar piya, jeevan diya ho...
zahar piya, jeevan diya <u>kitna udar tu</u> -2
aayo sharan tihari, bhole taar taar tu
kailash ke niwasi, namo bar bar hu
aayo sharan tihari, bhole taar taar tu

teri kripa bina naa hile ek bhi anu
lete hai swans teri daya se tanu tanu
kahe das ek bar mu-jhko nihar tu
aayo sharan tihari, bhole taar taar tu
kailash ke niwasi, namo bar bar hu
aayo sharan tihari, bhole taar taar tu

KAILASH KE NIWASI NAMO BAR BAR

dha	dhi	na	dha	tun	na	dha	dhi	na	dha	tun	na
1	2	3	4	5	6	1	2	3	4	5	6

GG GG GG GG GA^{b}GF FF DF   F   F   F
ek bel ptrm ek pushpm ek lota jl   ki dhar

GG B^{b}B^b B^b C'C'   B^{b}C'   FF   DF   F   F
dya lorij ke dete   hain-   chndra moli fal   char

 G G GG   G G GG   G GGG A^{b}GF
vyaghmbrm bhsmambrm jta jutli panch

C'B♭C' B♭B♭G   FF   G   FF   DF   FF
aasn   jmaye   baithe   hain kripa sindhu kailash

interlude:
FGC' C'B♭G E♭FG F G B♭B♭ C'C' B♭G GFF -2
FFF FFF E♭F E♭ C G E♭ G F -2

C E♭FF   F   FFF   FF E♭E♭ FGG G-   FF   E♭E♭ FGG G-F
kaila-sh ke nivasi   nmo bar ba-r hu- nmo bar ba-r hu-

GGC'   C'C'   B♭B♭G   GF   E♭F   GF   F
aayo   shrn tihari prbhu tar   tar tu -2

interlude:
E♭'E♭'E♭' F' E♭' C' B♭, C' B♭ GF G- 2
FFFFFF F E♭ C G E♭ G F -2

 GG   G B♭B♭   C' C'C'   C'B♭C' D' C'C'
bhkton ko kbhi shiv tune   nirash na kiya

 GG   C'C' B♭ B♭G   FE♭F   G FF
maga jinhe jo chaha vrdan   de diya

CE♭F   F   FF   FFF   B♭GF GFE♭ FCE♭C
bda- hai tera dayeja ho----

CE♭F   F   FF   FFF   FE♭ E♭FGG G-   FE♭ E♭FGG G-F
bda- hai tera dayeja bda data-r tu- bda data-r tu-

Vinod Kumar

GGC′ C′C′ B♭B♭G GF E♭F GF F
aayo shrn tihari prbhu tar tar tu -2

interlude:
F F E♭ – C E♭ G F – 2
GGC′ C′C′ B♭B♭G GF E♭F GF F -2

GGG B♭ B♭C′ C′   C′B♭ C′ D′C′ C′
bkhan kya kru main rakho ke dher ka

GGGC′   C′C′B♭   B♭ G   GFE♭ FGF F
chutki- bhbhut   me hai   khjana kuber ka

C   FF   FF   FF   FF   B♭GF GFE♭ FCE♭C
hai gang dhaar mukti dwaar ho-----

C   FF   FF   FF   FF
hai gang dhaar mukti dwaar

E♭E♭ FGG G-   FF   E♭E♭ FGG G-F
om ka-r tu- prbhu om ka-r tu-

GGC′ C′C′ B♭B♭G GF E♭F GF F
aayo shrn tihari prbhu tar tar tu -2

interlude: FGC′ C′B♭G E♭FG F G B♭B♭ C′C′ B♭G GFF -2
            FFF FFF E♭F E♭ C G E♭ G F -2

F G GB♭ B♭C′ C′ C′ B♭ C′D′C′ C′
kya kya nhi diya hai hm kya prman den

GG C'C'   B♭B♭G   GF   E♭F   GF F
bse gaye   trilok shmbhu tere dan se

CE♭F FF   FF   FF   B♭GF GFE♭ FCE♭C
zhr   piya jivn   diya ho----------------

CE♭F FF   FF   FF FFE♭   E♭FGG G- FFE♭   E♭FG G-F
zhr   piya   jivn diya kitna   uda-r tu- kitna   udar tu-

 GGC' C'C' B♭B♭G GF   E♭F GF   F
aayo   shrn tihari prbhu tar tar tu -2

interlude:
E♭'E♭'E♭' F' E♭' C' B♭, C' B♭ GF G- 2
FFFFFF F E♭ C G E♭ G F -2
FG GB♭ B♭C' C' C'C' B♭C' D' C'C'

FG GB♭   B♭C'   C' C'C' B♭C' D' C'C'
teri kripa bina   na hile ek bhi anu

GGC' C'   B♭B♭   GG FF   E♭ FG FF
lete   hain shwas teri dya se tnu tnu

CE♭   FF   FF   FF F-GE♭   E♭FG G- FGE♭   E♭FG G-F
kahe das   ek   bar mu-jhko nihar tu- mujhko nihar tu-

GGC'   C'C' B♭B♭G GF   E♭F GF   F
aayo-   shrn   tihari prbhu tar tar tu -2

Vinod Kumar

9. KO BIRHANI KO DUKH JANAI HO

Meera Bhajan   Singer: Lata Mangeshkar
Taal: Daadra   Chord: CE^{b}G   S=C

ko virahani ko dukh janai ho
meera ke pati aap ramaiya, dujo nahin koi chhanai ho
ko virahani ko dukh janai ho

rogi antar vaid basat hai, vaid hi aukhad jaanai ho

sab jag kudo kantak duniya, darad n koi pichhanai ho

ja ghat birha soi lakhi hai, kai koi hari jan manai ho

virah karad uri antar maanhi, hari bin sab sukh kaanai ho

dugdha aarat firai dukhari, surat basi sut manai ho

chaatak swati bund man maanhi, piv piv uktanai ho

meera ke pati aap ramaiya, dujo nahin koi chhanai ho

ghat= heart, harijan= hari bhakt, vaid= vaidya or krishna
aukhad= medicine, karad=kataar or knife, ur antar= in the heart
dagdh= burnt, aarat= grief, chaatag= chaatak bird, uklanai=
disturbed, daradh= pain, chhanai= protector

KO BIRHANI KO DUKH JANAI HO

dha	dhi	na	dha	tun	na	dha	dhi	na	dha	tun	na
1	2	3	4	5	6	1	2	3	4	5	6

prelude:

G C' ------------- C' B -------- A G ---- AGF$^\#$ ---- GE$^\flat$ ---- D – C –

aa ---

cores:

CD.BC E$^\flat$E$^\flat$D GGF$^\#$G C'C'B--- G ------ F$^\#$GF$^\#$E$^\flat$DC----

aa ---

E$^\flat$ CC.B.B E$^\flat$ CC CC C
ko virhini ko dukh jane ho

CE$^\flat$G B BB C'C' C'C'C' BB C'A GG GAF$^\#$-GF$^\#$ E$^\flat$
mira- ke pti aap rmaiya, duja nhin koii chha-----ne ho

E$^\flat$ CC.B.BF$^\#$ F$^\#$ CC CC C
ko virhini-- ko dukh jane ho

B ------- D' C'BAGFE$^\flat$E$^\flat$F$^\#$GBAGB$^\flat$ – AGA – E$^\flat$ F$^\#$ G B
um ---

.BE$^\flat$ F$^\#$F$^\#$F$^\#$ F$^\#$E$^\flat$F$^\#$ E$^\flat$CC .B F$^\#$E$^\flat$F$^\#$ F$^\#$ GGG GE$^\flat$AA G
rogi antr vai-d bst hai, vai-d hi okhd ja--ne ho

E$^\flat$E$^\flat$ F$^\#$G BC'C' BC'D$^{\flat'}$ C'C'C' BBB C' AG GGAF$^\#$-GF$^\#$ E$^\flat$
sb jg ku-do kntk duniya, drdh n koii pichha----ne ho

E$^\flat$ CC.B.BF$^\#$ F$^\#$ CC CC C
ko virhini-- ko dukh jane ho

F$^\#$ ------ B$^\flat$A ------ AGF$^\#$E$^\flat$E$^\flat$ ---- E F$^\#$ G ---
um ---

Vinod Kumar

C E♭G AAA AGF#E♭AGB BAG G
ja ght birha soii------- lkhi- hai,

G GA F#F#   F#E♭F#F# E♭-CD   C
kai koii hri   j---n ma---nai ho

F#E♭F# GGB BC' BC'E♭' D'C' BB BC' AA GG F#- GF# E♭
virh krd uri antr mahi, hri bin sb sukh ka--nai ho

E♭ CC.B.B E♭ CC   CC   C
ko virhini ko dukh jane ho

CE♭G B BB C'C' C'C'C' BB C'A GG GAF#-GF#   E♭
mira- ke pti aap rmaiya, duja nhin koii chha-----ne ho

10. MANGAL BHAWAN AMANGAL HARI

Film: Geet Gata Chal (1975) Music: Ravindra Jain
Lyrics: Ramcharit Manas, Singer: Jaspal Singh
Taal: Kaharwa Chord: GB^{b}D′ S=C#
Transpose +1 and play from C scale

mangal bhavan amangal haari,
drabahu su dasharath achar bihari
raam siya raam siya raam jai jai raam -2

ho, hoi hai wohi jo raam rachi raakha,
ko kari tarak badhave saakha, raam siya raam...

ho dheeraj dharam mitra aru naari
aapad kaal parakhiye chaari, raam siya raam...

ho, jehike jehi par satya sanehu
so tehi milay na kachhu sandehu, raam siya raam...

ho jaaki rahi bhawana jaisi
prabhu murati dekhi tin taisi
raam siya raam siya raam jai jai raam

ho raghukul reet sada chali aayi
praan jaaye par vachan na jaayi
raam siya raam siya raam jai jai raam

ho, hari anant hari katha ananta
kahahi sunahi bahuvidhi sab santa
raam siya raam siya raam jai jai raam

Vinod Kumar

MANGAL BHAWAN AMANGAL HARI

dhage	nati	nke	dhin	dhage	nati	nke	dhin	dhage	nati	nke	dhin	dhage	nati	nke	dhin
12	34	56	78	12	34	56	78	12	34	56	78	12	34	56	78

D'   D'E^b'D'   D'D'D'   D'D'E^b'C'D' B^{b}D'D' D'E^b'F'E^b'D'-C'-

ho mangl bhvn amangl   hari -------------

C'D'C'   B^b AAGA B^{b}AC' B^{b}A-G

drbhu su dsrth achr   bihari

 G   GA   C'   BA GA A A   G FD

ram siya ram siya ram jy jy ram - 2

G   GA AC'D' C'B GA A A   G

ram siya ra-m siya ram jy jy ram

D'   D'E^b'   D'D' D' D'E^b' C'D' AC'D'-D' D'E^b'F'E^b' D'-C'-

ho, hoihai vhi jo ram   rchi ra--- kha----------

C'D'   C'B^b AAG AB^{b}AC'B^b A-G-

ko   kre trk   bdhae--- sakha

D'   D'E^b'D' D'D'D' F'E' F'G' E^b'D' D'E^b'F'E^b' D'-C'-

ho, dhirj   dhrm mitr aru nari-----------

C'D'C'B^b A-G AB^{b}AC'B^b A-G-

aa-pd   kal prkhiye- chari

D'   D'D'E^b'D' D'D' D'D' E^b'C' D'B^{b}D'D' D'E^b'F'E^b'D'-C'-

ho, jehike jehi pr stya snehu-------------

C' B♭   AAG A B♭A   C'B♭A-G-
so tehi mily   n kchhu sndehu----

G   GA   C' BA GA A A G FD
ram siya ram siya ram jy jy ram -
music: D' – E' – D' E' G' – E' D' C' E' D' D' –

D'   D'E♭' D'D' D'E♭'C'D' B♭D'D' D'E♭'F'E♭'D'-C'-
ho, jaki   rhi bhavna jaisi------------

C'D'   C'B♭AA   GAB♭A   C'B♭ A-G-
prbhu mu-rti   de-khi- tin taisi

D'D'E♭'D' D'D' D'F'E'   F'G' E♭'D' D'E♭'F'E♭' D'-C'-
rghukul rit   sda   chli aaii

C'D'C' B♭AA GA B♭AC' B♭ A-G-
pra-n ja-e   pr vchn   n jaii

G   GA   C' BA GA A A G FD
ram siya ram siya ram jy jy ram -

D'   D'D' E♭'D'D' D'D' F'E'F'   G'E♭'D' D'E♭'F'E♭' D'-C'-
ho, hri annt   hri ktha-   annta

C'D'C' B♭AA GAB♭A   C'B♭ A-G-
kahhi sunhi bhuvidhi sb   snta

G   GA   C' BA GA A A G FD
ram siya ram siya ram jy jy   ram -

Vinod Kumar

11. MAN TARPAT HARI DARSHAN KO AAJ

Film: Baiju Bawra (1952)
Lyrics: Shakeel Badayuni
Taal: Teen Taal
Transpose +3 and play from C scale

Music: Naushad Ali
Singer: Md. Rafi
Chord: FA♭C′ S=D#

hari om hari om hari om hari om
man tarpat hari darshan ko aaj -2
more tum bin bigade sagare kaaj
ho, binti karat hoon rakhiyo laaj
man tarpat hari darshan ko aaj

tumare dwaar ka main hoon jogi -2 aa...
hamari oar nazar kab hogi
suno more vyaakul man ka baaj
man tarpat hari darshan ko aaj -2

bin guru gyaan kahaan se paaun -2 aa...
deejo daan hari gun gaaun
sab guni jan pe tumhara raaj
man tarpat hari darshan ko aaj -2

murli manohar aas na todo
dukh bhanjan mora saath na chhodo
mohe darshan bhiksha de do aaj

MAN TARPAT HARI DARSHAN KO AAJ

dha	dhin	dhin	dha	dha	dhin	dhin	dha	dha	tin	tin	ta	ta	dhin	dhin	dha
1	2	3	4	5	6	7	8	9	10	11	12	13	14	15	16
$.A^b$	$.B^b$	C	F	-	-	-	-	E^b	F	E^b	C	-	-	-	-
h	ri	om	-	-	-	-	-	h	ri	om	-	-	-	-	-
C	C	C′	-	-	-	-	-	A^b	B^b	A^b	F	-	-	-	-
h	ri	om	-	-	-	-	-	h	ri	om	-	-	-	-	-
						F	F	E^b	F	E^b	C	$.B^b$	C	$.A^b$	$.B^b$
						m	n	t	r	p	t	h	ri	d	r
C	F	F	F	E^b	F	F	F	E^b	F	A^b	B^b	C′	C′	C′	B^b
sh	n	ko	aa	-	j	mo	re	tu	m	bi	n	bi	g	re	-
A^b	B^b	A^b	F	-	F	E^bF	A^bB^b	C′	C′C′	C′B^b	C′	B^b	A^b	FA^b	B^bC′
s	g	re	ka	-	j	ho-	--	ho	bin	ti-	k	r	t	hun-	--
A^b	B^b	A^b	F	-	F	F	F	E^b	F	E^b	C	$.B^b$	C	$.A^b$	$.B^b$
r	khi	yo	la	-	j	m	n	t	r	p	t	h	ri	d	r
C	F	F	F	E^b	F	-	-	-	E^b	E^b	F	A^b	-	-B^b	B^b
sh	n	ko	aa	-	j	-	-	-	tu	m	re	dwa	-	-r	ka
C′	-	C′	-	$E^{b\prime}$	B^b	C′	-								
main	-	hun	-	jo	-	gi	-								

aa------ E^b F A^b B^b C′ ----- A^b F A^b B^b A^b F -----

C E^b F ---- E^b C $.A^b$ $.B^b$ C E^b F -------

									E^b	E^b	F	A^b	-	B^b	B^b
									tu	m	re	dwa	-	r	ka
C′	-	C′	-	$E^{b\prime}$	B^b	C′	-	-	C′	C′	C′	C′	-	B^b	A^b
main	-	hun	-	jo	-	gi	-	-	h	m	ri	o	-	r	n

Vinod Kumar

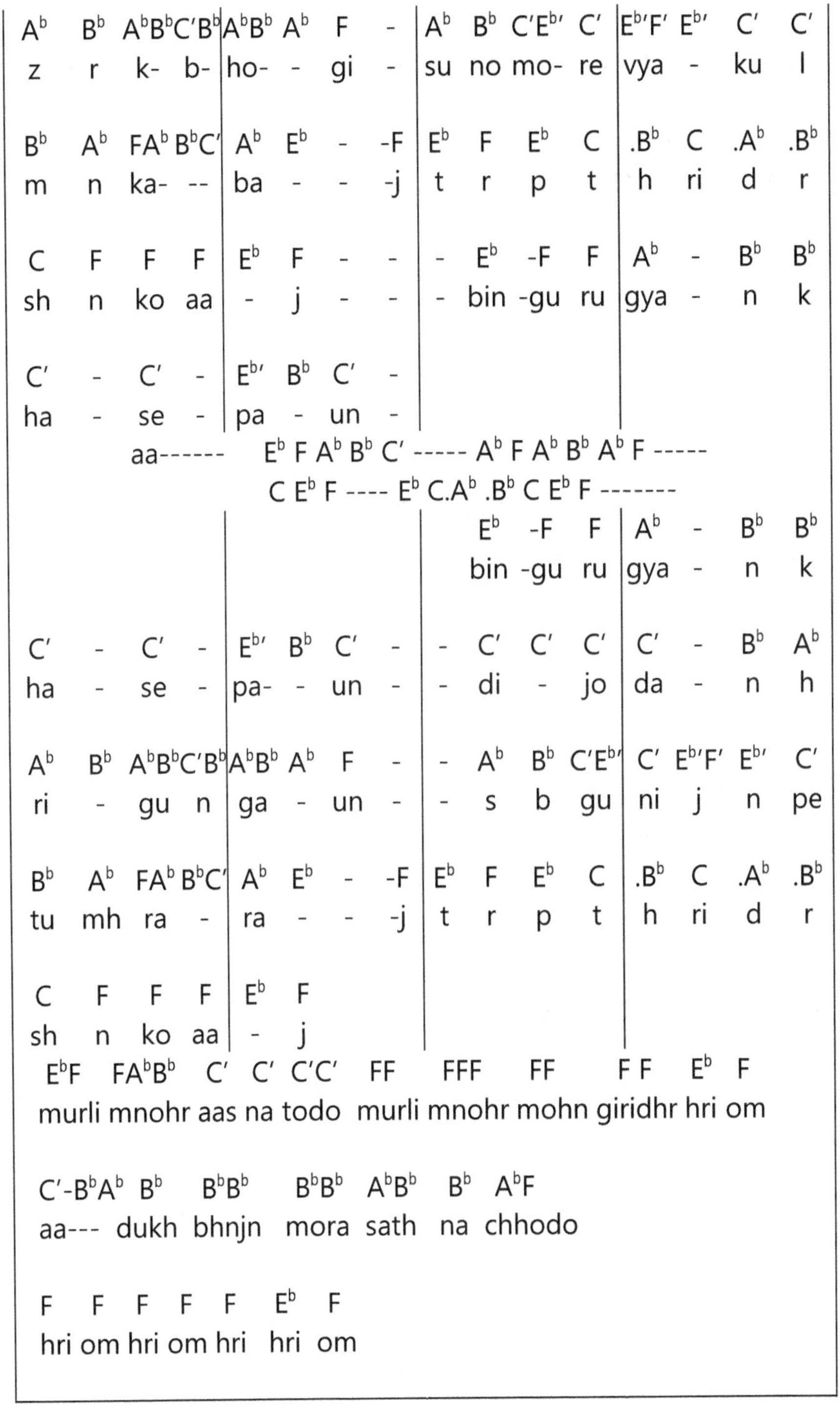

A♭	B♭	A♭B♭C′B♭	A♭B♭ A♭	F	-	A♭	B♭	C′E♭′	C′	E♭′F′ E♭′	C′	C′
z	r	k- b-	ho-	-	gi	-	su	no mo-	re	vya	-	ku	l

B♭	A♭	FA♭B♭C′	A♭	E♭	-	-F	E♭	F	E♭	C	.B♭	C	.A♭	.B♭
m	n	ka- --	ba	-	-	-j	t	r	p	t	h	ri	d	r

C	F	F	F	E♭	F	-	-	-	E♭	-F	F	A♭	-	B♭	B♭
sh	n	ko	aa	-	j	-	-	-	bin	-gu	ru	gya	-	n	k

C′	-	C′	-	E♭′	B♭	C′	-
ha	-	se	-	pa	-	un	-

aa------   E♭ F A♭ B♭ C′ ----- A♭ F A♭ B♭ A♭ F -----
C E♭ F ---- E♭ C.A♭ .B♭ C E♭ F -------

E♭	-F	F	A♭	-	B♭	B♭
bin	-gu	ru	gya	-	n	k

C′	-	C′	-	E♭′	B♭	C′	-	-	C′	C′	C′	C′	-	B♭	A♭
ha	-	se	-	pa-	-	un	-	-	di	-	jo	da	-	n	h

A♭	B♭	A♭B♭C′B♭	A♭B♭ A♭	F	-	-	A♭	B♭	C′E♭′	C′	E♭′F′	E♭′	C′
ri	-	gu n	ga	-	un	-	-	s	b	gu	ni	j	n	pe

B♭	A♭	FA♭B♭C′	A♭	E♭	-	-F	E♭	F	E♭	C	.B♭	C	.A♭	.B♭
tu	mh	ra	-	ra	-	-	-j	t	r	p	t	h	ri	d	r

C	F	F	F	E♭	F
sh	n	ko	aa	-	j

E♭F	FA♭B♭	C′	C′	C′C′	FF	FFF	FF	F F	E♭	F
murli mnohr aas na todo murli mnohr mohn giridhr hri om

C′-B♭A♭	B♭	B♭B♭	B♭B♭	A♭B♭	B♭	A♭F
aa--- dukh bhnjn mora sath na chhodo

F	F	F	F	F	E♭	F
hri om hri om hri hri om

F   A^{b}B^b C'E$^{b'}$ F' F'--   FF   FFF   FF   F F   E^b F
mohe drshn bhiksha de do-- murli mnohr mohn giridhr hri om

C'C'   C'F' E$^{b'}$C'   B^b A^b B^{b}C' B^b A^b F
mohe   drshn bhiksha de do aaj de do aaj

FF   FFF   FF   F F   E^b F
murli mnohr mohn giridhr hri om x5

A^b B^b B^b C' C' E$^{b'}$ E$^{b'}$ F'
hri om hri om hri om hri om

12. MAN RE TU KAAHE N DHEER DHARE

Film: Chitralekha (1964)   Music: Raushan
Lyrics: Sahir Ludhiyanvi   Singer: Md. Rafi
Taal: Kaharwa   Chord: EGC' S=C#
Transpose +1 and play from C scale

man re tu kaahe na dhiir dhare
vo nirmohii moh naa jaane,
jinakaa moh kare, man re ...

is jiivan kii chadhatii dhalatii, dhuup ko kisane baandhaa
rang pe kisane pahare daale, rup ko kisane baandhaa
kaahe ye jatan kare, man re ...

utanaa hii upakaar samajh koi, jitanaa saath nibhaa de
janama maran kaa mel hai sapanaa, ye sapanaa bisaraa de
koi na sang mare, man re ...

Vinod Kumar

MAN RE TU KAAHE N DHEER DHARE

dha	ge	n	ti	n	ke	dhi	n	dha	ge	n	ti	n	ke	dhi	n
1	2	3	4	5	6	7	8	1	2	3	4	5	6	7	8

prelude:
F A B^b C' D' E' E' C'   B^b D' F' E'
B^b D' E' E' C'   B^b D' C' F'
A B^b C' B^b A F flute: AGF E G F A – G F

 FF   AG G EGF   F EDE   FE---C
 mn   re- tu ka-he na dhi-r dhre

 C   E ^{D}E FEG   G-E F GAB^b-AG BBD'E'   F'E'C' AC'
 vo ni-r mo-hi mo-h na jane,   jinka-   mo-h kre

 flute: E'-D'C'-AF
      mn re ...

 C'C' E'D'E'F'E'   C'AC'   AAC'A C'C'C'
 is ji--vn ki--- chdhti- dhlti

 C'C'   C' E'D'C'- C'GGAB^b-A-
 dhup ko kisne- ban--------dha-

 C'-E'D' E' F'E'C'AC' AAC'-A C'C'
 rn—g- pe kisne--- phre--- dale

 C'C' C' E'D'C' C'GGAB^b-A
 rup ko kisne ban--------dha

 C'C' C' F'E'C' AC'
 kahe ye jtn   kre

 flute: E'-D'C'-AF
 mn re ...

C'C'E'D'E' F'E'   C'AC' A-C' AC'C' C'C'
utna---   hi-   u p---ka-r smjh koii

C'C'C' E'D'E'C' C'C'GGAB$^\flat$ A
jitna sa---th nibha-----   de

C'C'E'D' E'F'E'   C'AC' AC' A   C'C'C'
jnm-   mrn   ka--   mel hai spna

C'   C'C'C'E'D'E' C'C'C'GGAB$^\flat$-   A
ye spna----   bisra----------   de

C'C' C' F'E'C' AC'
koii n sn-g   mre

flute: E'-D'C'-AF

FF   AG G EGF   F EDE   FE---C
mn   re- tu ka-he na dhi-r dhre

Vinod Kumar

13. MURALIYA DE DO RADHA PYARI

Krishna Bhajan

Taal: Kaharwa

Singer: Juthika Roy, Kamal Das Gupta

Chord: DFB^b S=C#

Transpose +1 and play from C scale

https://www.youtube.com/watch?v=NJuS2pU22jQ&sns=em

muraliya de do radha pyari -2
muraliya main nahin linhi murari

baadal bin jaise mor niras aur chandra bina jaise rajani
vaise murali bin mohe murali vala kaun kahe re sajani
main nahin linhi murari, muraliya main nahin linhi murari

murali bin kaho kaise pyari, sukh dukh tumhein bhulaaun
ab maan lo mori kahi kar jorun, tumhein kabhi na sataaun, sataaun
tumhein kabhi na sataaun
main nahin linhi murari, muraliya main nahin linhi murari

main jaan gayi tumhri chaturaayi, murali main dungi kanhaai -2
mil jaaye poonam ko krishna salone, jhuthi baat banaayi banaayi
jhuthi baat banaayi
de do radha pyari, muraliya de do radha pyari

is murali ki dhun to naagar, nisdin mujhe rulaayi
madhuban mein sabhi kunjan mein, aisi kari chaturaayi
tune aisi kari chaturaayi
fir na rulaaun fir na sataaun, jo main murali paaun
dono milkar sab ke ghar ghar, prem ki jyot jalaaun jalaaun
prem ki jyot jalaaun
muraliya de do radha pyari, muraliya le lo krishna murari

MURALIYA DE DO RADHA PYARI

dha	ge	n	ti	n	ke	dhi	n	dha	ge	n	ti	n	ke	dhi	n
1	2	3	4	5	6	7	8	1	2	3	4	5	6	7	8

FGFGB^b A GF   FGFE^{b}D   E^b FF
murliya- de do- ra----dha- pya-ri

FGFGB^b A GF   FGFE^{b}D   E^b FF
murliya- de do- ra----dha- pya-ri

FGFGB^b A   GF   FGFE^{b}D   DE^{b}FF   F G B^b C'
murliya- main nhi   li---nhi   mura-ri   music

C'C'B^b D'C' B^{b}A   B^{b}B^b B^{b}A^{b}A^b GG
badl   bin jaise   mor nirs   aur

A^{b}A^b GA^b GF E^{b}GGF
chndra bina jaise rjni-

FF   AAA GA GF   E^{b}DE^b FGA^{b}G
vaise murli bin mohe murli   va—la-

C'C'   B^{b}AB^b A^{b}G   E^{b}GGF
kaun khe-   re-   sjni-

A   GF FGFE^{b}D   DE^{b}FF
main nhi li---nhi   mura-ri

FGFGB^b A   GF   FGFE^{b}D   DE^{b}FF
murliya- main nhi   li---nhi   mura-ri

music D E^b F G A^b G F D F

FFF   E^{b}E^b DC AF   GFF
murli   bin kaho kaise pyari

Vinod Kumar

GC'   B♭C'   AGA♭   GFDF
sukh dukh tumhe- bhulaun

FF   FG   B♭   B♭C'C'   C'C'B♭ C'E♭' D'C'C'
ab   maan lo mo-ri   kahi- kr   jo-run

C'C'D'   C'B♭A   G FGB♭B♭   B♭ AB♭ C' C'
tumhe- kbhi-   n sta-un   s ta-   - un

C'C'D'   C'B♭A   G FE♭GGF
tumhe- kbhi-   n sta-un-

A   GF   FGFE♭D   DE♭FF
main nhi li---nhi   mura-ri

FGFGB♭   A   GF FGFE♭D   E♭ FF
murliya- main nhi li---nhi   murari

G   A-G FG- FEF   E♭D DE♭FF
main ja-n gyi- tumhri chtu ra—ii

FGB♭ B♭   B♭C'C'   C'B♭C'C' B♭AGF
murli main dun-gi knhaii -------

FGB♭ B♭   B♭C'C'   C'B♭C'C'
murli main dun-gi knhaii

C'C' C'C'   C'B♭C' A♭ G-F   F FGA- GAB♭-
mil jae punm   ko krishna s lo---   ne---

B♭B♭   AG FE♭FF   FB♭AB♭A♭G
jhuthi bat bna-ii bna--- ii-

B♭B♭   AG FE♭GGF
jhuthi bat bna--ii

A GF   FGFE^{b}D   E^b FF
de do- ra----dha- pya-ri

FGFGB^b A   GF FGFE^{b}D   E^b FF
murliya- de do- ra----dha- pya-ri

D E^b F G A^b G F D F

FF   FFE^b DC DF   F FGA^b-GG
is   murli ki- dhun to nagr

GA^{b}GF   GAB^b C'C'B^b- A- G- F-
nisdin   mujhe--   rula--   ii -------

FGB^b B^b B^{b}B^b C'C'B^b B^{b}C'
mdhubn me sbhi   kunjn me-

C'C'   D'B^b AGFG E^{b}DC
aesi   kri   chturaii tune-

DF FFGA^b GA^{b}GF   G A B^b C'
aesi kri--   chturaii   music

C' C' D'E'F' E' E'   F'E^b'D'C'
fir n rulaun fir n   staun

B^b AG   AC'   C'D'E^b' D' D'C'
jo main- murli paun ----

C'C'   C'D'B^{b}B^b A   G FG   G
dono milkr   sb   ke ghr ghr

DE^{b}D   C DFF FFGG AGF
prem ki jyot jlaun   jlaun

DE♭D C DFF AGF
prem ki jyot jlaun

FGFGB♭ A GF FGFE♭D   E♭ FF
murliya- de do- ra----dha- pya-ri

FGFGB♭   A GF FGFE♭D   E♭ FF
murliya le lo kri----shna murari

14.   NA JI BHAR KE DEKHA N KUCHH BAT KI

Krishna Bhajan   Music: Vinod Agrawal
Lyrics: Vinod Agrawal   Singer: Vinod Agrawal
Taal: Daadra   Chord: DFA   S=C#
Transpose +1 and play from C scale

na jee bhar ke dekha na kuchh baat ki
badi aarzu thi mulaqat ki
karo drishti ab to prabhu karuna ki
badi aarzu thi mulaqat ki

gaye jab se mathura vo mohan murari,
sabhi gopiyaan brij mein vyakul thi bhaari
kahaan din bitaaya kahaan raat ki
badi aarzu thi mulaqat ki

chale aao ab to o pyare kanhaiya
yah sooni hai kunjan aur vyakul hai gaiya
suna do ab to inhein dhun murali ki,
badi aarzu thi mulaqat ki

ham baithe hain gam unka dil mein hi paale
bhala aise mein khud ko kaise sambhale
na unki suni na kuchh apni kahi,

badi aarzu thi mulaqat ki

tera muskurana bhala kaise bhulein
vo kadman ki chhaiyaan vo saavan ke jhule
na koyal ki ku ku na papihe ki pi
badi aarzu thi mulaqat ki

tamanna yahi thi ki aayeinge mohan,
main charnon mein vaarungi tan man yah jiivan
haay mera yah kaisa bigda naseeb
badi aarzu thi mulaqat ki

NA JI BHAR KE DEKHA N KUCHH BAT KI

dha	dhi	na	na	dhi	na	dha	dhi	na	na	dhi	na
1	2	3	4	5	6	1	2	3	4	5	6

```
D  F  E♭  C    DD    D   GG    FA   G
na ji  bhr ke dekha, na kuchh bat  ki


AB♭  GFF    E♭   E♭GFE♭   D
bdi  aarzu  thi, mulaqat  ki


DF   E♭C    D    D    DG     GFA  G
kro  drishti ab   to  prbhu  kruna ki


AB♭  GFF    E♭   E♭GFE♭   D
bdi  aarzu  thi, mulaqat   ki


B♭B♭  B♭B♭B♭  B♭   B♭AGB♭   A
bdi   aarzu  thi, mulaqat   ki
```

Vinod Kumar

AB♭ GFF   E♭   E♭GFE♭   D
bdi aarzu thi, mulaqat ki

C'C'   D'   D'   D'D'F'   F'   E♭'F' E♭'   D'D'D'
gaye jb   se mthura vo   mo-hn   murari

F'F'   F'   E'   F'F'F'   E♭'   C'F'   E♭'D'D'
gaye jb   se mthura vo mohn murari

E♭'E♭'   E♭'D'E♭'   E♭'   D'   B♭E♭'   D'   D'D'
sbhi gopiya   brij me vyakul thi bhari

B♭B♭C'   B♭AG   F   E♭   G F   E♭   DD
sbhi---   gopiya brij me vyakul thi bhari

DF   E♭   CDD   DG   FA G
kha din bitaya, kha   rat ki

AB♭ GFF   E♭   E♭GFE♭   D
bdi aarzu thi, mulaqat ki

C'C'   D'D' D' F' F' E♭'F' E♭'   D'D'D'
chle aao ab to o pya-re   knheya

F'F'   F'E' F'   F' F' C'F'   E♭'D'D'
chle   aao ab to o pya-re   knheya

E♭'   E♭'E♭'   D'   E♭'E♭'   D'   B♭E♭'   D'   D'D'
yh suni hai kunjn aur vyakul hai gaiya

B♭ B♭C'B♭   A   GF   E♭   G F   E♭   DD
yh suni   hai kunjn aur vyakul hai gaiya

DF   E♭   CD   D   D   G   FA   G
suna do inhe ab to dhun murli ki

AB^b GFF   E^b E^{b}GFE^b D
bdi aarzu thi, mulaqat ki

C'   C'D'   D'   D'   F'F'   E^b'F' E^b'   D'   D'D'
hm   baithe hain gm unka   dil me hi pale

F'   F'F'   E'   F'   F'F'   C'   F' E^b'   D'D'
hm baithe hain gm unka dil me hi   pale

E^b'E^b' E^b'D' E^b'   E^b'   D'   B^{b}E^b'   D' D'D'
bhla   aese me khud   ko kaise   smbhale

B^{b}B^{b}C' B^{b}A   G   F   E^b GF   E^b DD
bhla   aese me khud ko kaise   smbhale

 D F E^b CD   D   D   GGF   AG
na unki   suni na kuchh apni   khi

AB^b GFF   E^b E^{b}GFE^b D
bdi aarzu thi, mulaqat ki

C'C'   D' D' D' F'   F'E^b'F'   E^b'D'   D'D'
tera   muskurana bhla-   kaise bhule

F'F'   F' E' F'F'   E^b'C' F'E^b'   D'D'
tera   muskurana bhla kaise bhule

E^b' E^b' E^b'   D'   E^b'E^b'   D' B^{b}E^b'   D'   D'D'
vo kdmn   ki chhaiya, vo savn   ke jhule

B^b B^{b}C'B^b A   GF   E^b G F E^b DD
vo kdmn   ki chhaiya, vo savn ke jhule

D F E^b C D D   D   GGF   A   G
na koyl ki ku ku, na ppiha ki pi

Vinod Kumar

AB^b GFF E^b E^{b}GFE^b D
bdi aarzu thi, mulaqat ki

C'C'D' D'D' F' F' E^b'F'E^b'D'   D'D'
tmnna yhi thi ki   aa-enge mohn

F'F'F'   E'F'   F' F' C'F'E^b'   D'D'
tmnna yhi thi ki aaenge   mohn

E^b'   E^b'E^b' D' E^b'E^b'D' B^b E^b' D' D'D'
main chrno me varungi   tn mn yh jivn

B^b B^{b}C'B^b A   GFE^b G F E^b DD
main chrno   me varungi tn mn yh jivn

D   FE^b C   DD   D GGGF   AG
hay mera yh kaisa hai bigda- nsi---b

AB^b GFF   E^b E^{b}GFE^b D
bdi aarzu thi, mulaqat ki

15. NI MAIN NACHNA MOHAN DE NAAL

Krishna Bhajan   Chord: F#ADb'   S=C#
Taal: Kaharwa Dugun
Transpose +1 and play from C scale

ni main nachna mohan de naal aaj mainu nach lain de
nach lain de ni mainu nach lain de
ni main nach ke manana dildaar aaj mainu nach lain de

duniya de lai nacheya bathera, fir vi na koi banya mera
ki karna, jay ho -2
ki karna hai ae sansaar aaj mainu nach lain de
ni main nachna mohan de naal aaj mainu nach lain de

pairaan de vich ghungru bann ke, apne shyam di jogan ban ke
ni main nach ke, jay ho -2
ni main nach ke manana nandlaal aaj mainu nach lain de
ni main nachna mohan de naal aaj mainu nach lain de

satguru ne ae rasta dikhaya, baanke bihaari ton mainu milaaya
aise satguru te, -2
aise satguru te main balihaar, aaj mainu nach lain de
ni main nachna mohan de naal aaj mainu nach lain de

vrindavan vich jaavan de lai, pyar mohan da paavan de lai
sune baanvari ne, -2
sune baanvari ne taane hazaar, aaj mainu nach lain de
ni main nachna mohan de naal aaj mainu nach lain de

Vinod Kumar

NI MAIN NACHNA MOHAN DE NAAL

dhage	nti	nke	dhin	dhage	nti	nke	dhin	dhage	nti	nke	dhin	dhage	nti	nke	dhin
12	34	56	78	12	34	56	78	12	34	56	78	12	34	56	78

prelude:

F# A F# E F#-A-AAA, F# A F# E F#-A-AAA
F# A F# E F#-AAC'BA, F# A F# E F#-A-AAA
D'AB - B D'C'A, ABF# AC'- B- AA-
AAA AF#A BC'BC', B--- BD^{b'} D^{b'} D^{b'}
BD^{b'} BA A

A A   EF#F#A E' E'   A A EF#F#A   E' E'
ni main nachna jy ho ni main nachna jy ho
                                                          A   A
                                                          ni main

E   F#F# A   A   A   - BC' BC' B   -   -   B   D^{b'} D^{b'} D^{b'} D^{b'}
n   chna -   mo hn - de- --   na -   -   l   a   j   main nu

B   D^{b'} B   A   A   -   -   -   D^{b'} E' E' E' F#' F#' F#' F#'
n   ch   lai n   de -   -   -   n   ch lai n   de ni main nu

B   C'   B   C'   B   A   A   A   E   F#F# A   E' E' -   A   A
n   ch   lai n   de -   ni main n chke -   jy ho -   ni main

E   F#F# A   E' E' -   A   A   E   F#F# A   A   A   A   C' -
n   chke -   jy ho -   ni main n chke -   m   na na dil -

B   -   -   -   D^{b'} D^{b'} D^{b'} D^{b'} B   D^{b'} B   A   A   -   A   A
da -   -   r   a   j   main nu   n   ch lai n   de -   ni main

E   F#F# A   A   A   -   BC' BC' B   -   -   B   D^{b'} D^{b'} D^{b'} D^{b'}
n   chna -   mo hn -   de- --   na -   -   l   a   j   main nu

B   D^{b'} B   A   A   -   -   -
n   ch lai n   de -   -   -
interlude:

E′ E′ E′ F#′ E′ F#′ E′-
C′ C′ C′ B A B A-
E F# A E′ Db′---
C′ C′ C′ B A B A-

																E′	E′	E′
																du	ni	ya
F#′	-	F#′	-		B	C′	B	C′		A	B	B	A		-	E′	E′	E′
de	-	l	ii		n	ch	ya	b		the	-	ra	-		-	fi	r	vi
E′	F#′	F#′	-		B	C′	B	C′		A	B	B	A		E′	D′	C′D′	B
na	-	ko	ii		b	n	ya	-		me	-	ra	-		-	-	-	-
A	-	A	-		E	F#F#	A	E′		E′	-	A	-		E	F#F#	A	E′
-	-	ki	-		k	rna	-	jy		ho	-	ki	-		k	rna	-	jy
E′	-	A	-		E	F#F#	A	A		A	-	C′	-		B	-	-	B
ho	-	ki	-		k	rna	-	hai		ae	-	sn	-		sa	-	-	r
Db′	Db′	Db′	Db′		B	Db′	B	A		A	-	A	A		E	F#F#	A	A
a	j	main	nu		n	ch	lai	-n		de	-	ni	main		n	chna	-	mo
A	-	BC′	BC′		B	-	-	B		Db′	Db′	Db′	Db′		B	Db′	B	A
hn	-	de-	--		na	-	-	l		a	j	main	nu		n	ch	lai	n
A	-	-	-															
de	-	-	-															

E′E′   E′F#′ F#′F#′   BC′BC′   AB BA
pairan de-   vich   ghunghru-   bnn ke-

E′E′E′   E′F#′F#′   F#′ BC′BC′ AB BA   E′ D′ C′D′B- A
apne   shyam   di jo-gn   bn ke-   music

A A EF#   F#A   E′ E′ A A EF#   F#A   E′ E′
ni main nch   ke-,   jy ho, ni main nch   ke-,   jy ho

Vinod Kumar

A A   EF# F#A AF#A BC'B- Db'Db' Db'Db' BDb' BA A
ni main nch ke- mnana nndlal aaj   mainnu   nch lain de

A A   EF#F#A   AA BC'BC' BB D'D' D'D' BD' BA A
ni main nchna- mohn de---- nal aaj mainu nch lain de

E'E'E'E' F#' F#' BC'B C'ABBA
stguru ne   ae   rasta dikha-ya-

E'E'   E'E'F#'F#' F#'   BC'B   C'ABBA
banke biha-ri   ton   main-nu   mila-ya-

AA EF#F#A   A AA EF#F#A   A
aese stguru   te aese stguru   te

AA EF#F#A   A A   BC'B- Db'Db' Db'Db' BDb' BA A
aese stguru   te main blihar aaj   mainu nch lain de

A A   EF#F#A   AA BC'BC' BB Db'Db' Db'Db' BDb' BA A
ni main nchna- mohn de--- nal aaj mainu   nch lain de

E'E'E'F#'   F#'F#' BC'BC' AB BA
vrindavn   vich ja-vn de- laii

E'   E'E'F#' F#' BC'BC' AB BA
pyar mohn da pa-vn de- laii

AA E-F#A   A AA E-F#A   A
sune ban-vri ne sune ban-vri ne

AA E-F#A   A AB C'B- Db'Db' Db'Db' BDb' BA A
sune ban-vri ne tane hzar aaj   mainu   nch lain de

A A   EF#F#A AA BC'BC' BB D'D' D'D' BD' BA A
ni main nchna- mohn de--- nal aaj mainu nch lain de

16.   O DUNIYA KE RAKHWALE

Film: Baiju Bawra (1952)   Music: Naushad Ali
Lyrics: Shakeel Badayuni   Singer: Md. Rafi
Taal: Kaharwa   Chord: CEG   S=C#
Transpose +1 and play from C scale

bhagavaan, bhagavaan.... bhagavaan
o duniya ke rakhavaale, <u>sun dard bhare mere naale</u>-2
aas niraas ke do rango se, duniya tune sajaai
nayyaa sang tufaan banaayaa, milan ke saath judaai
jaa dekh liyaa harajaai
o... lut gayi mere pyaar ki nagari, <u>ab to nir bahaa le</u>-2
o.... ab to nir bahaa le
o duniya ke rakhavaale, sun dard bhare mere naale...

aag bani saavan ki barkha, phul bane angaare
naagan ban gayi raat suhaani, patthar ban gaye taare
sab tut chuke hai sahaare
o jivan apanaa vaapas le le, jivan dene vaale o
o duniya ke rakhavaale

chaand ko dhundhe paagal suraj shaam ko dhundhe saveraa
mai bhi dhundhu us pritam ko ho na sakaa jo mera
bhagavaan bhalaa ho teraa
o qismat phuti aas na tuti paanv me pad gaye chhaale
o duniya ke rakhavaale

mahal udaas aur galiyaan suni chup chup hai divaarein
dil kyaa ujadaa duniya ujadi ruth gai hain bahaarein
ham jivan kaise guzaarein
o mandir girataa phir ban jata, dil ko kaun sambhaale

Vinod Kumar

o duniya ke rakhavaale

o duniya ke rakhavaale, sun dard bhare mere naale

sun dard bhare mere naale

o duniya ke rakhavaale..., rakhavaale...

rakhavaale... rakhavaale......

O DUNIYA KE RAKHWALE

dha	ge	n	ti	n	ke	dhi	n	dha	ge	n	ti	n	ke	dhi	n
1	2	3	4	5	6	7	8	1	2	3	4	5	6	7	8

D E E..... F#
bh g va..... n

E F# AGAG – F# E D C
bh g va ....n

D F# F#.... E   sitar : C D E D E -----
bh g va.... n

														C	D
														o	-
D	E	E	-	E	-	D	D	E	F#	F#	A	G	-	G	G
du	ni	ya	-	ke	-	r	kh	va	-	le	-	-	-	su	n
G	A	A	F#	F#	-	E	D	E	F#	F#	-	-	-	E	D
d	r	d	bh	re	-	me	re	na	-	le	-	-	-	su	n
D	E	E	E	D	C	D	F#	F#	-	E	-	C	D	E	F#
d	r	d	bh	re	-	me	re	na	-	le	-				
A	F#	C	D	E	-										
E	F#	F#	F#	F#	-	F#	E	D	-	F#	E	D	-	C	.B
aa	-	s	ni	ra	-	s	ke	do	-	rn	-	gon	-	se	-

D	F#	E	D	C	-	C	D	D	E	E	-	-	-	-	-
du	ni	ya	-	tu	-	ne	s	ja	-	yi	-	-	-	-	-
-	E	-	F#	G	G	A	-	A	-	B	B	B	-	B	-
-	nai	-	ya	sn	g	tu	-	fa	-	n	b	na	-	ya	-
B	C'	-	D'	B	-	A	A	BC'	E'	E'	-	-	-	D'E'	F#'
mi	l	n	ke	sa	-	th	ju	da-	-	ii	-	-	-	ja	-
F#'	-	F#'	F#'	E'	D'	C'	D'	D'	E'	E'	-	-	-	E'	D'
de	-	kh	li	ya	-	h	r	ja	-	ii	-	-	-	o	o
F#'	F#'F#'	F#'	F#'	F#'	-	E'	F#'	A'	G'	G'	A'	F#'	F#'	E'	-
o	lut	g	ii	me	-	re	-	pya	-	r	ki	n	g	ri	-
D'	E'	E'	-	E'	-	E'	D'	E'	F#'	F#'	-	-	-	-	-
a	b	to	-	ni	-	r	b	ha	-	le	-	-	-	-	-
-	D'	E'	E'	E'	F#'	E'	D'	E'	F#'	F#'	G'	-	-	-	-
-	a	b	to	ni	-	r	b	ha	-	le	-	-	-	-	-
E'	-	-	D'	-	-	C'	-	-	B	-	-	A	-	B	-
o															
B	C'	B	A	F#	A	B	B	A	G	-	A	F#	-	-	-
a	b	to	-	ni	-	r	b	ha	-	-	-	le	-	-	-
E'	-	-	D'	-	-	C'	-	D'	F#'	-	-	-	-	C	D
-	-	-	-	-	-	-	-	-	-	-	-	-	-	o	-
D	E	E	-	E	-										
du	ni	ya	-	ke	-										
D	E	F#	G	B	-	-	A	G	E	D	E	-	-	-	-

Vinod Kumar

D	E	E	E	E	-	EF$^\#$	E	D	D	.B	C	D	E	E	-
aa	-	g	b	ni	-	sa	-	v	n	ki	-	b	r	kha	-

D	G	G	A	F$^\#$	-	E	D	D	E	G	F$^\#$	E	-	-	-
fu	-	l	b	ne	-	an	-	ga	-	-	-	re	-	-	-

-	A	-B	-B	C'	C'	D'	D'	-	E'	-E'	-E'	E'	-	E'	-
-	na	-g	-n	b	n	g	yi	-	ra	-t	-su	ha	-	ni	-

-	D'	D'	D'	E'	D'	F$^{\#}$'	E'	C'	-	-	D'	B	-	D'	E'
-	pt	th	r	b	n	g	ye	ta	-	-	-	re	-	s	b

D'E'	F$^{\#}$'	F$^{\#}$'	F$^{\#}$'	E'	D'	C'	D'	D'	E'	E'	-	-	-	E'	D'
tu-	-	t	chu	ke	-	hain	s	ha	-	re	-	-	-	o	o

F$^{\#}$'	F$^{\#}$'	-F$^{\#}$'	F$^{\#}$'	F$^{\#}$'	F$^{\#}$'	E'	F$^{\#}$'	A'	G'	G'	A'	F$^{\#}$'	-	E'	-
o	ji	-v	n	a	p	na	-	va	-	p	s	le	-	le	-

E'	-	D'	-	C'	D'	D'	B	B	C'B	A	F$^\#$	A	B	A	-
-	-	-	-	-	-	-	-	ji	-v	n	de	-	ne	-	-

G	-	-	A	F$^\#$	-	E	D	D	E	E	-	D	C	D	F$^\#$
va	-	-	-	le	-	o	-	du	ni	ya	-	ke	-	r	kh

F$^\#$	E	E	-	E	F$^\#$G	A	BC'	D'	E'F$^{\#}$'	G'	-	E'D'	C'	-	D'
va	-	le	-	-	-	-									

-	E'	-	-	D'	B	G	A	F$^\#$	-	E	-				

-	E	F$^\#$A	A	A	B	B	C'	A	-	G	-	F$^\#$	-	E	E
-	chan	-d	ko	dhun	-	dhe	-	pa	-	g	l	su	-	r	j

-	E	F$^\#$	F$^\#$	F$^\#$	-	F$^\#$	E	F$^\#$	B	G	-	-	-	-	-
-	sha	-m	ko	dhun	-	dhe	s	ve	-	ra	-	-	-	-	-

-	-	-	-	-	-	-	-	-	E	G	G	G	A	A	-
-	-	-	-	-	-	-	-	-	main	-	bhi	dhun	-	dhu	-
F#	G	F#	E	F#	D	E	-	E	-	C'	C'	C'	-	D'	-
u	s	pri	-	t	m	ko	-	ho	-	n	s	ka	-	jo	-
C'	-	B	-	-	-	E'	E'	E'	F#'	F#'	F#'	E'	D'	C'	D'
me	-	ra	-	-	-	bh	g	va	-	n	bh	la	-	ho	-
D'	E'	E'	-	-	-	E'	D'	F#'	F#'F#'	F#'	F#'	F#'	-	E'	F#'
te	-	ra	-	-	-	o	o	o	kis	m	t	fu	-	ti	-
A'	G'	G'	A'	F#'	-	E'	-	E'	-	D'	-	C'	D'	D'	B
aa	-	s	n	tu	-	ti	-	-	-	-	-	-	-	-	-
-	B	C'	A	F#	A	B	A	G	-	-	A	F#	-	E	D
-	paa	v	me	p	d	g	ye	chha	-	-	-	le	-	o	-
D	E	E	-	D	C	D	F#	F#	E	E	-	-	-		
du	ni	ya	-	ke	-	r	kh	va	-	le	-	-	-		
E'	-	-	-	D'E'	F#'E'	F#'	-	-	D'	E'	-	C'	-A	B	-
aa	-	-	-	-	-	-	-	-	-	-	-	-	-	-	-
B	-	-	A	B	-	-	G	-	-	F#	-	-	E	-	-
aa	-	-	-	-	-	-	-	-	-	-	-	-	-	-	-
A	B	-	-	C'	B	-	D'	C'	-	-	-	E'	-	-	-
aa	-	-	-	-	-	-	-	-	-	-	-	-	-	-	-
E'	-	-	-	D'E'	F#'E'	F#'	-	-	D'	E'	-	C'	-A	B	-
aa	-	-	-	-	-	-	-	-	-	-	-	-	-	-	-
-	BC'	A	B	F#	-F#	A	A	BC'	C'	D'	-	-	C'	-	B
-	mh	l	u	da	-s	au	r	gli	yan	-	-	-	su	-	ni

Vinod Kumar

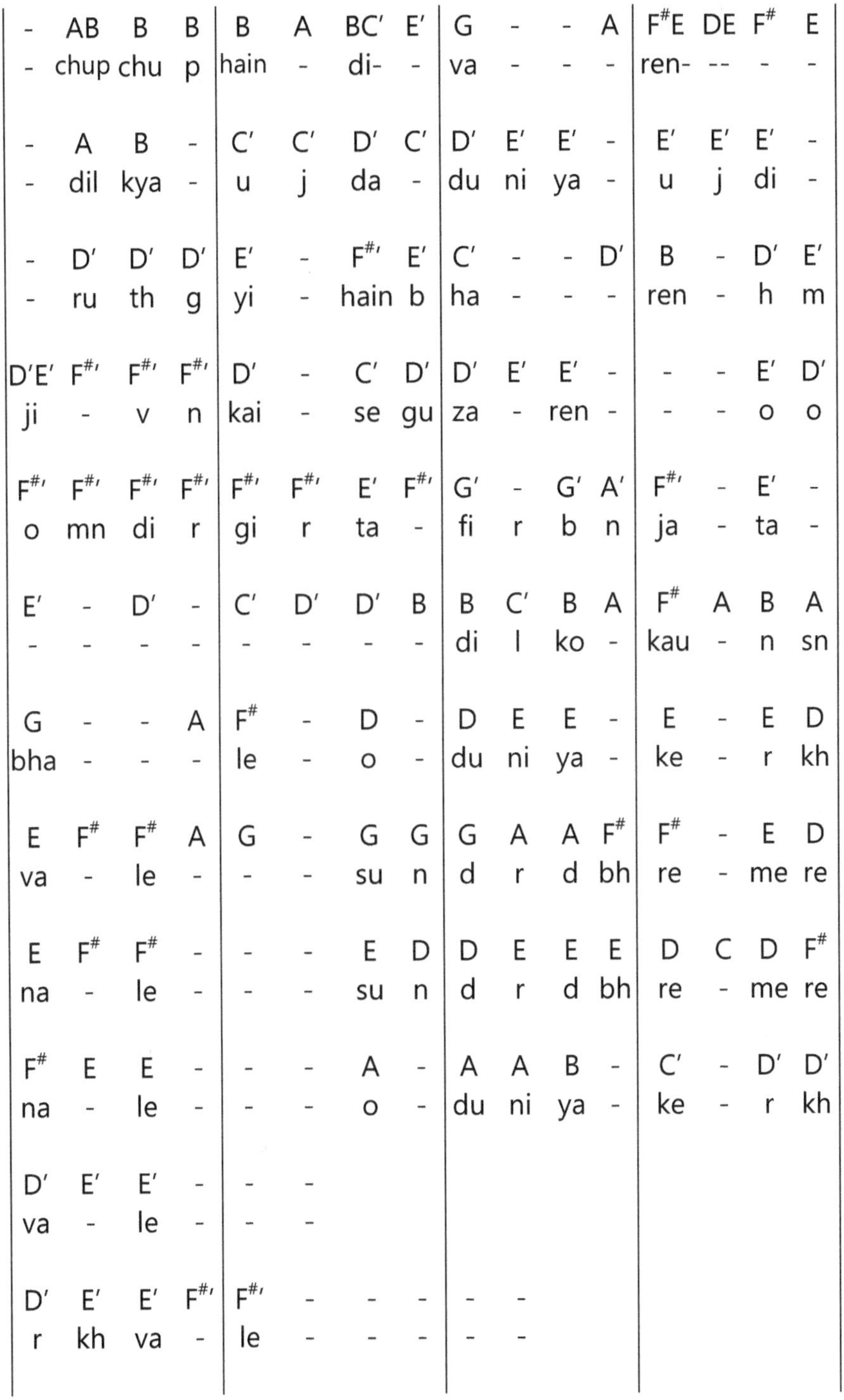

-	AB	B	B	B	A	BC'	E'	G	-	-	A	F#E	DE	F#	E
-	chup	chu	p	hain	-	di-	-	va	-	-	-	ren-	--	-	-
-	A	B	-	C'	C'	D'	C'	D'	E'	E'	-	E'	E'	E'	-
-	dil	kya	-	u	j	da	-	du	ni	ya	-	u	j	di	-
-	D'	D'	D'	E'	-	F#'	E'	C'	-	-	D'	B	-	D'	E'
-	ru	th	g	yi	-	hain	b	ha	-	-	-	ren	-	h	m
D'E'	F#'	F#'	F#'	D'	-	C'	D'	D'	E'	E'	-	-	-	E'	D'
ji	-	v	n	kai	-	se	gu	za	-	ren	-	-	-	o	o
F#'	F#'	F#'	F#'	F#'	F#'	E'	F#'	G'	-	G'	A'	F#'	-	E'	-
o	mn	di	r	gi	r	ta	-	fi	r	b	n	ja	-	ta	-
E'	-	D'	-	C'	D'	D'	B	B	C'	B	A	F#	A	B	A
-	-	-	-	-	-	-	-	di	l	ko	-	kau	-	n	sn
G	-	-	A	F#	-	D	-	D	E	E	-	E	-	E	D
bha	-	-	-	le	-	o	-	du	ni	ya	-	ke	-	r	kh
E	F#	F#	A	G	-	G	G	G	A	A	F#	F#	-	E	D
va	-	le	-	-	-	su	n	d	r	d	bh	re	-	me	re
E	F#	F#	-	-	-	E	D	D	E	E	E	D	C	D	F#
na	-	le	-	-	-	su	n	d	r	d	bh	re	-	me	re
F#	E	E	-	-	-	A	-	A	A	B	-	C'	-	D'	D'
na	-	le	-	-	-	o	-	du	ni	ya	-	ke	-	r	kh
D'	E'	E'	-	-	-										
va	-	le	-	-	-										
D'	E'	E'	F#'	F#'	-	BC'	-	-	-	-					
r	kh	va	-	le	-	-	-	-	-	-					

E′	F#′	F#′	G′	G′	-	-	-	-	-	
r	kh	va	-	le	-	-	-	-	-	
F#′	G′	G′	A′	A′	-	-	-	-	-	
r	kh	va	-	le	-	-	-	-	-	

17.   OH RE TAAL MILE NADI KE JAL ME

Film: Anokhi Raat (1968)
Lyrics: Indeevar
Taal: Kaharwa

Music: Raushan
Singer: Mukesh
Chord: EA♭B S=C

oh re taal mile nadi ke jal men, nadi mile saagar men
saagar mile kaun se jal men, koi jaane na

suraj ko dharati tarase, <u>dharati ko chndrama-2</u>
paani men siip jaise <u>pyaasi har atma-2</u>
o mitwa re …. paani men siip jaise pyaasi har atma
bund chhupi kis baadal men koi jaane na

anajaane hothhon par kyon <u>pahachaane git hain-2</u>
kal tak jo begaane the, <u>janmon ke mit hai-2</u>
o mitwa re …. kal tak jo begaane the, janmon ke mit hai
kya hoga kaun se pal men koi jaane na

Vinod Kumar

OH RE TAAL MILE NADI KE JAL ME

dha	ge	n	ti	n	ke	dhi	n	dha	ge	n	ti	n	ke	dhi	n
1	2	3	4	5	6	7	8	1	2	3	4	5	6	7	8

prelude: E .B EF E EF E EF E x 4
ho ha, hii re hii re hii re x 4

E .B E – A♭ A B A♭ A – B A A♭ - - A♭ G
ho ha, hun ....

E – A♭ A B A♭ A – B A A♭ –
hun ....

											A♭	-	A♭	-
											o	h	re	-
G	A♭	A♭	A	-	A	A	-	A♭	A♭	-	A♭	A♭	-	E	-
ta	-	-	-	l	mi	le	-	n	di	-	ke	j	l	me	-
-	-	E	A♭	-	A♭	A♭	-	A♭	-	A	-	B	-	-	-
-	-	n	di	-	mi	le	-	sa	-	gr	-	me	-	-	-
-	-	B	C'	-	B	C'	-	A	-	C'	B	A	-	A♭	-
-	-	sa	gr	-	mi	le	-	kau	-	n	se	j	l	me	-
-	-	A	B	-	A	-	A	A♭	-	-	-	A♭	-	A♭	-
-	-	ko	ii	-	ja	-	ne	na	-	-	-	o	h	re	-
G	A♭	A♭	A	-	A	A	-	A♭	A♭	-	A♭	A♭	-	E	-
ta	-	-	-	l	mi	le	-	n	di	-	ke	j	l	me	-

interlude:
B ----------- B B C' D' E' E' – B –
E' – C' D' – C' B – A –
AC'BA F – E –, A♭ABA♭A – B A A♭-,
BAA♭- BAA♭- BAA♭- BAA♭-

		B	-	A	-	A	-	A♭	-	A♭	-	A♭	-	A♭	-
		su	-	r	j	ko	-	dh	r	ti	-	t	r	se	-

A	-	A	-	A	-	A	-	A♭	-	-	A♭	A♭	-	G	-
-	-	dh	r	ti	-	ko	-	chn	-	-	dr	ma	-	-	-
-	-	E	-	B	-	A	-	A♭	-	-	A♭	A♭	-	-	-
-	-	dh	r	ti	-	ko	-	chn	-	-	dr	ma	-	-	-
-	-	B	-	A	-	A	-	A♭	-	-	A♭	A♭	-	A♭	A
-	-	pa	-	ni	-	me	-	si	-	-	p	jai	-	se	-
B	-	B	-	A	-	A♭	-	A♭	-	-	A♭	A♭	-	G	-
-	-	pya	-	si	-	h	r	aa	-	-	t	ma	-	-	-
-	-	E	-	A♭	-	A♭	-	A♭	-	-	A♭	A♭	-	-	-
-	-	pya	-	si	-	h	r	aa	-	-	t	ma	-	-	-
-	-	-	A♭	A♭	A♭	A	-	B	-	-	C'	B	-	-	C'
-	-	-	o	mi	t	va	-	re	-	-	-	-	-	-	-
B	-	-	C'	B	C'	E'	-	-	-	E'	-	D'	-	C'	-
-	-	-	-	-	-	-	-	-	-	pa	-	ni	-	me	-
B	-	-	A	A	-	A	-	-	-	D'	-	C'	-	B	-
si	-	-	p	jai	-	se	-	-	-	pya	-	si	-	h	r
A	-	-	C'	B	-	-	-	-	-	C'	-	C'	C'	C'	-
aa	-	-	t	ma	-	-	-	-	-	bun	-	d	chhu	pi	-
A	A	C'	-	A	-	A♭	-	-	-	A	C'	-	A	-	A
ki	s	ba	-	d	l	me	-	-	-	ko	ii	-	ja	-	ne
A♭	-	-	-	A♭	-	A♭	-	G	A♭	A♭	A	-	A	A	-
na	-	-	-	o	h	re	-	ta	-	-	-	l	mi	le	-
A♭	A♭	-	A♭	A♭	-	E	-	-	-	E	A♭	-	A♭	A♭	-
n	di	-	ke	j	l	me	-	-	-	n	di	-	mi	le	-

Vinod Kumar

Ab	-	A	-	B	-	-	-	-	-	B	C'	-	B	C'	-
sa	-	gr	-	me	-	-	-	-	-	sa	gr	-	mi	le	-
A	-	C'	B	A	-	Ab	-	-	-	A	B	-	A	-	A
kau	-	n	se	j	l	me	-	-	-	ko	ii	-	ja	-	ne
Ab	-	-	-	Ab	-	Ab	-	G	Ab	Ab	A	-	A	A	-
na	-	-	-	o	h	re	-	ta	-	-	-	l	mi	le	-
Ab	Ab	-	Ab	Ab	-	E	-								
n	di	-	ke	j	l	me	-								

18. RAKH LAAJ MERI GANPATI

Ganpati Bhajan
Lyrics: Hari Om Sharan
Taal: Rupak

Music: Hari Om Sharan
Singer: Hari Om Sharan
Chord: DFA   S=C

rakh laaj meri ganpati, apanee sharan mein leejie.

kar aaj mangal ganapati, apanee kripa ab keejie.

rakh laaj meri ganpati...

siddhi vinaayak duhkh haran, santaap haaree sukh karan.

karoon praarthana main nitt prati, varadaan mangal deejie.

rakh laaj meri ganpati....,

teree daya, teree krpa, he naath ham maange sada.

tere dhyaan mein khove mati, pranaam mam ab leejie.

rakh laaj meri ganpati...,

karate pratham tav vandana, tera naam hai dukh bhanjana.

karana prabhu meree shubh gati, ab to sharan me leejie.

rakh laaj meri ganpati...,

RAKH LAAJ MERI GANPATI

ti	ti	na	dhi	na	dhi	na	ti	ti	na	dhi	na	dhi	na
1	2	3	4	5	6	7	1	2	3	4	5	6	7

```
DDEA  FGE  DA-G  C'A   AAD'  D'D♭'D'  E'D♭'  D'---  AC'C'A
sumirn di-p  jlaii    ke--,  krun-  hridy   me-   dhya-------n


D♭'D'C'  AGD  E  FGD  EED  C.A  .AC    D♭D♭D--
shrn     pde- ki la-j  rkh-,  he- mere  bhgvan
```

Vinod Kumar

prelude:
E G C'—G A D'-- C' A F E—
D E F --- A E D GFED .A D GFED .A D

												G	E
												r	kh
Dᵇ	-	D	C	-	.A	-	D	D	Dᵇ	D	-	G	E
la	-	j	me	-	ri	-	g	n	p	ti	-	a	p
A	-	A	C'	B	D'	-	A	C'	A	G	E	G	E
ni	-	sh	r	n	me	-	li	-	ji	e	-	k	r
Dᵇ	-	D	C	-	.A	.A	D	D	Dᵇ	D	-	G	E
aa	-	j	mn	-	g	l	g	n	p	ti	-	a	p
A	-	A	C'	B	D'	D'	A	C'	A	G	E	G	E
ni	-	kri	pa	-	a	b	ki	-	ji	e	-	r	kh
Dᵇ	-	D	C	-	.A	-	E	E	Dᵇ	D	-		
la	-	j	me	-	ri	-	g	n	p	ti	-		

interlude: sitar:
F A – F – E D EFDE A- G C'- A-
FFFA – FG- E D EFDE A- G C'- A-
flute: A E' D' ---- C'BAG A G F G E D
sitar: A- A- F G – E-D- EFDE A- G C'- A-

												G	A
												si	-
C'	-	B	C'	-	G	A	C'	C'	B	C'	C'	A	-
dhi	-	vi	na	-	y	k	du	kh	h	r	n	sn	-
A	E'	E'	E'	-	D'	-	D'	Dᵇ'	D'	C'	A	A	-
ta	-	p	ha	-	ri	-	su	kh	k	r	n	sn	-

D'	-	D'	A	F	D	E	F	F	E	D	D	G	E
ta	-	p	ha	-	ri	-	su	kh	k	r	n	k	run

D^b	-	D	C	-	.A	-	D	D	D^b	D	-	G	E
pra	-	rth	na	-	main	-	ni	t	pr	ti	-	v	r

A	-	A	C'	B	D'	D'	G	A	G	E	-	G	E
da	-	n	mn	-	g	l	di	-	ji	e	-	r	kh

D^b	-	D	C	-	.A	-	E	E	D^b	D	-		
la	-	j	me	-	ri	-	g	n	p	ti	-		

GAC' BC' GAC' BC'   A AE'E' E'D' D'D$^{b'}$ D'C'A
te-ri   dya, te-ri kripa, he na-th hm mange sda-

A D'D' AF   DEF   ED
he nath hm man-ge sda

GE D^{b}D   C   .AD   D^{b}D   GEAA C'B D'D' GAGE-
tere dhyan me khove mti, prnam mm ab   li-jie-

GE D^{b}D C.A EED^{b}D
rkh laj meri gnpti
interlude: as above

GAC' BC'C' GA C'-BC' AA AE'E' E'D' D'D' D^b'D'C'A
krte prthm tav vndna,   tera na-m hai- dukh bhnjna-

GAC' E'E'D'
krte   krte

GAC' BC'C' GA C'-BC' AA AE'E' E'D' D'D' D^b'D'C'A
krte prthm tav vndna, tera na-m hai- dukh bhnjna-

AA D'D' AF DE   F- ED
tera nam hai- dukh bhn-jna

GED^b DC   .G.A   DD   D^bD   GE A AC'B D'   GAGE-
krna prbhu   meri shubh gti,   ab   to shrn   me   li-jie-

GE   D^bD   C.A   EED^bD
rkh   laj   meri   gnpti   (flute: at some places AC'—C'E'D'D^bD')

19. RAM CHARAN CHIT LAAI RE

Hari Bhajan   Singer: Prem Bhushan ji
Taal: Daadra   Chord: DGB   S=C#
Transpose +1 and play from C scale
https://www.youtube.com/watch?v=YBgYXVLL7Al

ek hi baan pran hari linha, deen jaan tehi nij pad deenha
(killed taadka rakshasi)
jab jab mara tab tab tara, bhakton ko to prabhu tera hi sahaara-2
han han
jab jab mara tab tab tara, bhakton ko to prabhu tera hi sahaara
shyam ho chahe raghurai re
han han shyam ho chahe raghurai re, bhajo radhe govinda
ram charan chit layi re bhajo radhe govinda
bhaktan ke sukhdaayi re bhajo radhe govinda

ek ayodhya dhaam me aaya ek mathura ka bhag badhaya
kyon bharat ko deenhi badaayi re
han haan bharat ko deenhi badaayi re bhajo radhe govinda
ram charan chit layi re bhajo radhe govinda
bhaktan ke sukhdaayi re bhajo radhe govinda

saryu kinare ek dhanua chalave jamuna kinare ek dhenu charaye-2
han han

saryu kinare ek dhanua chalave jamuna kinare ek dhenu charaye
saadhu, uu bhaye jagat ke saanyi re
han han uu bhaye jagat ke saanyi re bhajo radhe govinda
ram charan chit layi re bhajo radhe govinda
bhaktan ke sukhdaayi re bhajo radhe govinda

jan prahlad ko hari ne bachaya arjun ko sat gyan sikhaya-2
han han
jan prahlad ko hari ne bachaya arjun ko sat gyan sikhaya
ho, sab vidhi liinhi apnaayi re
ho, sab vidhi liinhi apnaayi re bhajo radhe govinda
ram charan chit layi re bhajo radhe govinda
bhaktan ke sukhdaayi re bhajo radhe govinda

jo jan gaave sab kuchh paave ant samay prabhu ur ko jaaye-4
maine bhi neh lagaayi re
han han maine bhi neh lagaayi re bhajo radhe govinda
ram charan chit layi re bhajo radhe govinda
bhaktan ke sukhdaayi re bhajo radhe govinda

prem se bolo jay siya rama
shri avadh me jay siya rama
sarju kinaare jay siya rama
gokul bhawan me jay siya rama
hare ram ji jay siya rama
prem se bolo jay siya rama
ram charan chit layi re bhajo radhe govinda
bhaktan ke sukhdaayi re bhajo radhe govinda

Vinod Kumar

RAM CHARAN CHIT LAAI RE

dha	dhi	na	dha	tun	na	dha	dhi	na	dha	tun	na
1	2	3	4	5	6	1	2	3	4	5	6

DD D EF# GG GG GAGF#E
ek hi ban pran hri linha---

F#D EF#E F#F#   F#F# GF# EF#D
diin ja-n tehi nij pd dinha

BA BA GF#E DE EE EE F#F#F#G
jb jb mara-, tb tb tara, bhkton-

F# E ED CC D DDD
ko to prbhu tera hi shara

 B B BA BA GF#E DE EE EE
ha ha jb jb mara-, tb tb tara,

F#F#F#G   F# E ED CC D DDD
bhkton-   ko to prbhu tera hi shara

GG   G F#F# EECD   DF#E
shyam ho chahe rghuraii re---

E EG GG G F#F#   EECD   DF#E EE CDE   EDD
(ha ha) shyam ho chahe rghuraii re-- bhjo radhe- govinda

GG   GF#F# EE CD DF#E EE CDE   EDD
ram chrn chit layi re--- bhjo radhe- govinda

GGG F# EECD DF#E EE CDE   EDD
bhktn ke sukhdaii re--- bhjo radhe- govinda

BAB AGG DEE E EE F#F# F#GF#E   ED CD DDD
ek ayodhya dha-m me aaya ek mthura- ka- bhag bdhaya

GGG G F#E   DCD DF#E
bhrt ko dinhi bdaii re ---

G G GGG G F#E   DCD   DF#E   EE CDE   EDD
ha ha bhrt ko dinhi bdaii re --- bhjo radhe- govinda

GG   GF#F# EE CD DF#E   EE   CDE   EDD
ram chrn   chit layi re--- bhjo radhe govinda

GGG   F# EECD   DF#E   EE CDE   EDD
bhktn ke sukhdaii re--- bhjo radhe- govinda

BAB AGG GG DEE   EEE   F#F#F#   GF#E EE CDD   DDD
sryu kinare ek dhnuaa chlave jmuna   kinare ek dhe-nu   chrae

G G
ha ha

BAB AGG GG DEE   EEE F#F#F#   GF#E EE CDD   DDD
sryu kinare ek dhnuaa chlave jmuna   kinare ek dhe-nu   chrae

 G G   GF#F# E CD DF#E
uu bhye jgt   ke saii re—

E G G G   GF#F# E CD DF#E   EE CDE   EDD
ha ha uu bhye jgt   ke saii re— bhjo radhe- govinda

GG   GF#F# EE CD DF#E EE   CDE   EDD
ram chrn   chit layi re--- bhjo radhe govinda

GGG   F# EECD   DF#E   EE CDE   EDD
bhktn ke sukhdaii re--- bhjo radhe- govinda

BA BAGG G DE E   EEE   F#F#G F# EE CDD   DDD
jn prhlad ko hri ne bchaya arjun ko st gyan sikhaya

Vinod Kumar

```
EG  B  BA BAGG  G  DE  E  EEE    F#F#G  F#   EE CDD   DDD
ha  ha jn  prhlad  ko  hri ne bchaya arjun  ko  st  gyan  sikhaya


EG   GG  GG   F#F#   EECD  DF#E
ho,  sb  bidhi  linhi    apnaii re---


EG   GG  GG   F#F#   EECD  DF#E   EE  CDE      EDD
ho,  sb  bidhi  linhi    apnaii re---  bhjo radhe-   govinda


GG   GF#F#   EE   CD  DF#E    EE   CDE     EDD
ram  chrn      chit  layi re---   bhjo  radhe  govinda


GGG   F#  EECD    DF#E   EE   CDE      EDD
bhktn  ke  sukhdaii re---   bhjo radhe-   govinda


BA  BA  GG  DE  EE    EE    F#F#  GF#E  EE    CD  D  DD
jo-  jn  gave sb  kuchh pave ant   smy   prbhu  ur  ko jaye


GG     G   F#E  ECD  DF#E
maine  bhi  neh  lgaii   re----


EEG    GG    G   F#E  ECD  DF#E   EE  CDE      EDD
haha-, maine bhi  neh  lgaii re----  bhjo radhe-   govinda


C-        D   DD   C  CD  DD
prem     se  bolo  jy siya rama


C-   DD  D    C  CD  DD
shri avdh me     jy siya rama


CC    DDD    C  CD  DD
srzu kinare    jy siya rama


continue repeat this -- C CD DD
then play this  E EF#  F#F#
```

E- F#- E- F#-
B- B- B- B-
D'- D'- D'- D'-

GG GF#F# EE CD DF#E EE CDE EDD
ram chrn   chit layi re--- bhjo radhe govinda

20. SHYAM PIYA MORI RANG DE

Meera Bhajan
Taal: Kaharwa
Transpose +1 and play from C scale

Singer: Anoop Jalota
Chord: DFA GB♭D'   S=C#

shyam piya mori rang de chunariya

aisee rang de ke rang naahin chhute,
dhobiya dhoye chaahe saari umariya

laal na rangaau main haree na rangaaun,
apne hi rang mein rang de chunariya

bina rangaaye main to ghar naahin jaaungi
beet hi jaaye chahe saari umariya

meera ke prabhu giridhar naagar
prabhu charanan mein laagi nazariya

Vinod Kumar

SHYAM PIYA MORI RANG DE

dha	ge	n	ti	n	ke	dhi	n	dha	ge	n	ti	n	ke	dhi	n
1	2	3	4	5	6	7	8	1	2	3	4	5	6	7	8

AA A   AAB♭A   B♭B♭   B♭ B♭AB♭GB♭   D'C' AGB♭   AAAA
rng de chunriya rng de chunriya-   rng de-- chunriya

AB♭   C' B♭A G GA B♭ AG F FG A GF E
rng de rng de rng de rng de rng de rng de

GF DCE   DDDD
rng de--- chunriya

FF   GB♭ GFE GF E DDDD
shyam piya mo-ri rng de chunriya

GA B♭ B♭C'B♭G   GF E DDDD
rng de chunriya   rng de chunriya

B♭B♭G B♭B♭   B♭ D' D'C' D'B♭ AA
aesi- rng   de, ke rng nahi chhute

D'D'D'   D♭'D'   AG FG AGAFE
dhobhiya dhoye chahe sari umriya-

B♭B♭ B♭ GB♭B♭   B♭ D'D' C' B♭AA
lal na rngaun main, hri na rngauu

D'D'D' D' D♭'D' AG FF G AGAFE
apne hi rng me- rng de chunriya-

AB♭C' C'B♭B♭   A A AA B♭C' B♭B♭A
bina   rngaye main to ghr nahi jaungi

D'D' D' D♭'D' AG FG AGAFE
biit hi jae chahe sari umriya

B♭B♭G B♭   B♭B♭   D'C'D'B♭ AAA
mira   ke prbhu giridhr   nagr

D'D'   D'D'D♭'D' AG   FG AGAFE
prbhu chrnn   me- lagi nzriya

D'D' B♭ AAAA
rng de chunriya x 8

Vinod Kumar

21. SHRI RAMCHANDRA KRIPALU

Shri Ram Stuti
Lyrics: Tulasidas
Taal: Rupak

Chord: .BDF$^{\#}$ DF$^{\#}$A   S=C#
Transpose +1 and play from C scale

shri ram chandra kripalu bhaju mana harana bhavabhaya darunam
navakanj lochana kanjamukh kara kanjapada kanjaarunam

kandarpa aganeeta ameeta chabi nava neela neeraja sundaram
patapeeta maanahu tarita ruchi-suchi naumi janaka sutaavaram

bhaju deena bandhu dinesha daanava daitya-vansha-nikandam
raghunanda aanand kanda kaushala chanda dasharatha nandanam

sira mukuta kundala tilak chaaru udaaru anga vibhushanam
aajaanubhuj sar chapadhara sangraama-jita-khara dushnam

iti vadati tulsidas shankara shesh muni mana ranjanam
mama hridaya kanj nivaas kuru kaamaadi khaladal ganjanam

man jaahi raachyo milahi so var sahaj sundar saanvaro
karuna nidhaan sujaan sheel saneh jaanat ravaro

ehi bhanti gauri asees suni siya sahit hiya harshit ali
tulasi bhavaanihi puji puni puni mudit man mandir chali

so: jaani gauri anukuul siya hiya harashu n jaai kahi
    manjul mangal muul baam ang farkan lage

SHRI RAMCHANDRA KRIPALU

ti	ti	na	dhi	na	dhi	na	ti	ti	na	dhi	na	dhi	na
1	2	3	4	5	6	7	1	2	3	4	5	6	7
												D	.B
												shri	-
D	-	E	F#	G	F#	E	D	-	E	F#	G	F#	E
ra	-	m	chn	-	dr	kri	pa	-	lu	bh	ju	m	n
D	E	E	D	D	D	.B	D	-	E	F#	-	F#	F#
h	r	n	bh	v	bh	y	da	-	ru	nm	-	n	v
F#	-	E	F#	A	A	A	A♭	-	A♭	F#	F#	E	D
kn	-	j	lo	-	ch	n	kn	-	j	mu	kh	k	r
D	E	D	D	E	F#	G	F#	-	E	D	-	D	.B
kn	-	j	p	d	kn	-	ja	-	ru	nm	-	kn	-
D	-	E	F#	G	F#	E	D	D	E	F#	G	F#	E
d	-	rp	a	g	ni	t	a	mi	t	chh	vi	n	v
D	E	E	D	-	D	.B	D	-	E	F#	-	F#	F#
ni	-	l	ni	-	r	j	sun	-	d	rm	-	p	t
F#	-	E	F#	A	A	A	A♭	A♭	A♭	F#	F#	E	D
pi	-	t	ma	-	n	hu	t	di	t	ru	chi	shu	chi
D	E	D	D	E	F#	G	F#	-	E	D	-	D	.B
nau	-	mi	j	n	k	su	ta	-	v	rm	-	bh	ju
D	-	E	F#	G	F#	E	D	-	E	F#	G	F#	E
di	-	n	bn	-	dhu	di	ne	-	sh	da	-	n	v
D	E	E	D	-	D	.B	D	-	E	F#	-	F#	F#
dai	-	tya	vn	-	sh	ni	kn	-	d	nm	-	r	ghu

Vinod Kumar

F#	-	E	F#	A	A	A	A♭	-	A♭	F#	F#	E	D
nn	-	d	aa	-	nn	d	kn	-	d	kau	-	sh	l
D	E	D	D	E	F#	G	F#	-	E	D	-	D	.B
chn	-	dr	d	sh	r	th	nn	-	d	nm	-	si	r
D	D	E	F#	G	F#	E	D	D	E	F#	G	F#	E
mu	ku	t	kun	-	d	l	ti	l	k	cha	-	ru	u
D	E	E	D	-	D	.B	D	-	E	F#	-	F#	-
da	-	ru	an	-	g	vi	bhu	-	sh	nm	-	aa	-
F#	-	E	F#	A	A	A	A♭	-	A♭	F#	F#	E	D
ja	-	nu	bhu	j	sh	r	cha	-	p	dh	r	sn	-
D	E	D	D	E	F#	G	F#	-	E	D	-	D	.B
gra	-	m	ji	t	kh	r	du	-	sh	nm	-	i	ti
D	D	E	F#	G	F#	E	D	-	E	F#	G	F#	E
v	d	ti	tu	l	si	-	da	-	s	shn	-	k	r
D	E	E	D	D	D	.B	D	-	E	F#	-	F#	F#
she	-	sh	mu	ni	m	n	rn	-	j	nm	-	m	m
F#	F#	E	F#	A	A	A	A♭	-	A♭	F#	F#	E	D
hri	d	y	kun	-	j	ni	va	-	s	ku	ru	ka	-
D	E	D	D	E	F#	G	F#	-	E	D	-	D	.B
ma	-	di	kh	l	d	l	gn	-	j	nm	-	m	nu
D	-	E	F#	G	F#	E	D	D	E	F#	G	F#	E
ja	-	hi	ra	-	che	u	mi	l	hin	so	-	v	ru
D	E	E	D	-	D	.B	D	-	E	F#	-	F#	F#
s	h	j	sun	-	d	r	san	-	v	ro	-	k	ru

```
F#  -   E  │ F#  A  │ A   A  │ Ab  -   Ab │ F#  -  │ E   D
na  -   ni │ dha -  │ n   su │ ja  -   n  │ si  -  │ lu  s

D   E   D  │ D   E  │ F#  G  │ F#  -   E  │ D   -  │ D   .B
ne  -   h  │ ja  -  │ n   t  │ ra  -   v  │ ro  -  │ e   hi

D   -   E  │ F#  G  │ F#  E  │ D   -   E  │ F#  G  │ F#  E
bhan -  ti │ gau -  │ ri  a  │ si  -   s  │ su  ni │ si  y

D   E   E  │ D   D  │ D   .B │ D   -   E  │ F#  -  │ F#  F#
s   hi  t  │ hi  y  │ h   r  │ shi -   a  │ li  -  │ tu  l

F#  -   E  │ F#  A  │ A   A  │ Ab  -   Ab │ F#  F# │ E   D
si  -   bh │ va  -  │ ni  hi │ pu  -   ji │ pu  ni │ pu  ni

D   E   D  │ D   E  │ F#  G  │ F#  F#  E  │ D   -  │
mu  di  t  │ m   n  │ mn  -  │ di  r   ch │ li  -  │
```

F#---------------- E ---------- F# ----------
jani gauri anukul siy hiy hrshu n jaii khi

E ------------ D   E F#E   DD
mnjul mngl mul bam ang frkn lge

Chord: DF#A --
bolo siyavr ram chndra ki jy, pvn sut hnuman ki jy

Chord: DF#A --
bolo bhaii sb sntn ki jy, jy jy sita ram jy jy radhe shyam

Vinod Kumar

22. SATGURU MAIN TERI PATANG

Taal: Kaharwa   Chord: DFA   S=C#
Transpose +1 and play from C scale

sat guru main teri patang, baba main teri patang
hawa vich ud di jawangi -2
saaiyaan dor hatthon chhadi na main katti jawangi

badi mushkil de naal mileya <u>mainu tera dwaraa ae</u>-2
mainu ikko tera aasra, <u>naale tera sahara ae</u>-2
hun tere hi bharose <u>hawa vich ud di jawangi</u>-2
saiyaan dor hatthon chhadi na main katti jawangi

aina charna kamla naalo <u>mainu dur hatai na</u>-2
is jhoothe jag de andar <u>mera pecha layi na</u>-2
je kat gayi taa sat guru <u>phir main lutti jawangi</u>-2
saiyaan dor hatthon chhadi na main, katti jawangi

ajj malleya buhaa aake <u>main tere dware da</u>-2
hatth rakh de ik baari tu <u>mere sir te pyaara da</u>-2
fir janam maran de gehde tau <u>main bachdi jawangi</u>-2
saiyaan dor hatthon chhadi na main katti jawangi

SATGURU MAIN TERI PATANG

dha	ge	n	ti	n	ke	dhi	n	dha	ge	n	ti	n	ke	dhi	n
1	2	3	4	5	6	7	8	1	2	3	4	5	6	7	8
												D	D	D	E
												s	t	gu	ru
C	-	-	D	D	F	E	-	D	-	-	D	D	-	D	-
main	-	-	te	ri	-	p	-	tn	-	-	g	ba	-	ba	-
C	-	-	D	D	F	E	-	D	-	D	D	D	A	A	A
main	-	-	te	ri	-	p	-	tn	-	g	h	va	-	vi	ch
A	A	A	-	G	-	$F^{\#}$	-	G	-	-	D	D	A	A	A
u	d	di	-	ja	-	van	-	gi	-	-	h	va	-	vi	ch
A	A	A	-	G	-	$F^{\#}$	-	G	-	-	-	G	-	G	$F^{\#}$
u	d	di	-	ja	-	van	-	gi	-	-	-	sa	ii	ya	-
G	A	-	G	G	-	F	-	F	-	G	-	E	-	D	C
do	-	-	r	h	t	tho	-	chh	d	di	-	na	-	main	-
E	-	E	-	F	-	E	-	D	-	-	-				
k	-	tti	-	ja	-	van	-	gi	-	-	-				
														A	A
														b	di
A	A	A	C'	C'	-	B	-	A	-	A	-	-	-	A	A
mu	sh	ki	l	de	-	na	l	mi	l	ya	-	-	-	main	nu
G	A	-	G	F	-	F	G	G	A	-	-	-	-	F	E
te	ra	-	d	va	-	ra	-	hai	-	-	-	-	-	main	nu
E	E	-	F	G	F	E	-	D	-	-	-	-	-	A	A
te	ra	-	d	va	-	ra	-	hai	-	-	-	-	-	main	nu

Vinod Kumar

A	-	A	C'	C'	-	B	-	A	-	-	A	A	-	A	A
i	-	kko	-	te	-	ra	-	aa	-	-	s	ra	-	na	le

G	A	-	G	F	-	F	G	G	A	-	-	-	-	F	E
te	ra	-	s	ha	-	ra	-	hai	-	-	-	-	-	na	le

E	E	-	F	G	F	E	-	D	-	-	-	-	-	D	D
te	ra	-	s	ha	-	ra	-	hai	-	-	-	-	-	hu	n

C	-	D	-	F	-	E	-	D	-	D	-	-	-	D	D
te	-	re	-	hi	-	bh	-	ro	-	se	-	-	-	hu	n

C	-	D	-	F	-	E	-	D	-	D	D	D	A	A	A
te	-	re	-	hi	-	bh	-	ro	-	se	h	va	-	vi	ch

A	A	A	-	G	-	$F^{\#}$	-	G	-	-	-	G	-	G	$F^{\#}$
u	d	di	-	ja	-	van	-	gi	-	-	-	sa	ii	ya	-

G	A	-	G	G	-	F	-	F	-	G	-	E	-	D	C
do	-	-	r	h	t	tho	-	chh	d	di	-	na	-	main	-

E	-	E	-	F	-	E	-	D	-	-	-
k	-	tti	-	ja	-	van	-	gi	-	-	-

```
AA    A-AC'  C'-B  AA  AA      GAA  GFFG  GA
aena chr-na- kmla nalon mainu  du-r htavi- na-

FE      EE  FGFE      D
mainu dur  htavi-     na

AA  A-AC'   C'B B  AA    AA  GAG   FFG  GA
is  jhu-the- jg  de andr mera  pecha  lavii- na-

FE      EEF  GFE D
mera pecha- lavii- na
```

D CC DDF E D-D-   DA A   AA GF#G
je kt gyi- ta stguru 2,   fer main lutti javangi 2,

GGF# GAG   GF   FG   E   DC   EE FED
saiiya   do-r hatho chhddi na, main- ktti javangi

AA A-AC'   C'-B AA   A   GA GF-G   GA
ajj   maleya   bu-ha aake main tere dwa-r   da-

FE   EEF   GFE   D
main- tere- dwa-r da

AA AA AC' C'B AA   A   AA   GA AG F-G GA
hth rkh de- ek   vari tun mere sir te- pyar da-

FE   E   EF   GFE D
mere sir   te- pyar da

D CC DDF FE   D-D-   DA A   AAA GF#G
fir jnm mrn   de-   ge-de- 2 to- main bchdi javangi 2,

GGF#   GAG   GF   FG   E   DC   EE FED
saiiya   do-r hatho chhddi na, main- ktti javangi

Vinod Kumar

23.   SUR KI GATI MAIN KYA JAANU

Music: Naresh Battacharya   Singer: Mukesh

Taal: Kaharwa   Chord: .A^bCE^b S=C#

Transpose +1 and play from C scale

sur ki gati main kya janu ek bhajan karna janu -2

arth bhajan ka bhi ati gehra usko bhi main kya janu-2

prabhu prabhu prabhu karna janu -2 naina jal bharna janu

sur ki gati main kya janu ek bhajan karna janu

sur ki gati main kya janu

gun gaye, gun gaye prabhu nyay na chhode

fir kyon tum gun gaate ho -2

main bola main prem deewana -2 itni baaten kya janu

sur ki gati main kya janu ek bhajan karna janu

sur ki gati main kya janu

SUR KI GATI MAIN KYA JAANU

dha	ge	na	ti	n	ke	dhi	n	dha	ge	na	ti	n	ke	dhi	n
1	2	3	4	5	6	7	8	1	2	3	4	5	6	7	8
E^b	E^b	FG	A^b	G	F	E^b	-	E^b	-	C	D^b	F	-	-	-
su	r	ki-	-	g	ti	main	-	kya	-	ja	-	nu	-	-	-
$.B^b$	-	C	C	D^b	-	D^b	-	C	-	$.G$	$.B^b$	$.A^b$	-	-	-
e	-	k	bh	j	n	k	r	na	-	ja	-	nu	-	-	-
E^b	-	E^b	C	E^b	E^b	F	-	A^b	-	A^b	A^b	G	B^b	A^b	-
a	r	th	bh	j	n	ka	-	bhi	-	a	ti	g	h	ra	-
A^b	C'	C'	-	C'	$D^{b\prime}$	C'	B^b	B^b	G	G	B^b	A^b	-	-	-
u	s	ko	-	bhi	-	main	-	kya	-	ja	-	nu	-	-	-
E^b	A^b	A^b	A^b	A^b	A^b	A^b	G	F	G	G	F	E^b	-	-	-
pr	bhu	pr	bhu	pr	bhu	k	r	na	-	ja	-	nu	-	-	-
$.B^b$	-	C	-	D^b	D^b	D^b	-	C	-	$.G$	$.B^b$	$.A^b$	-	-	-
nai	-	na	-	j	l	bh	r	na	-	ja	-	nu	-	-	-
E^b	E^b	FG	A^b	G	F	E^b	-	E^b	-	C	D^b	F	-	-	-
su	r	ki-	-	g	ti	main	-	kya	-	ja	-	nu	-	-	-
$.B^b$	-	C	C	D^b	-	D^b	-	C	-	$.G$	$.B^b$	$.A^b$	-	-	-
e	-	k	bh	j	n	k	r	na	-	ja	-	nu	-	-	-
E^b	E^b	FG	A^b	G	F	E^b	-	E^b	-	C	D^b	F	-	-	-
su	r	ki-	-	g	ti	main	-	kya	-	ja	-	nu	-	-	-
G	G	G	A^b	A^b	-	-	-	-	-	G	A^b	G	F	E^b	-
gu	n	ga	-	ye	-	-	-	-	-	-	-	-	-	-	-

G	G	G	-	A^b	-	A^b	A^b	G	-	A^b	G	F	E^b	E^b	-
gu	n	ga	-	ye	-	pr	bhu	nya	-	y	n	chho	-	de	-

$.B^b$	E^b	E^b	-	E^b	F	$F^\#$	F	E^{bF}	-	D^b	C	$.B^b$	-	-	-
fi	r	kyo	-	tu	m	gu	n	ga	-	te	-	ho	-	-	-

$.A^b$	-	D^b	-	D^b	-	C	-	D^b	F	-	F	G	-	A^b	-
main	-	bo	-	la	-	main	-	pre	-	m	di	va	-	na	-

A^b	C'	C'	-	C'	$D^{b'}$	C'	B^b	B^b	-	G	B^b	A^b	-	-	-
i	t	ni	-	ba	-	ten	-	kya	-	ja	-	nu	-	-	-

E^b	E^b	FG	A^b	G	F	E^b	-	E^b	-	C	D^b	F	-	-	-
su	r	ki-	-	g	ti	main	-	kya	-	ja	-	nu	-	-	-

$.B^b$	-	C	C	D^b	-	D^b	-	C	-	$.G$	$.B^b$	$.A^b$	-	-	-
e	-	k	bh	j	n	k	r	na	-	ja	-	nu	-	-	-

E^b	E^b	FG	A^b	G	F	E^b	-	E^b	-	C	D^b	F	-	-	-
su	r	ki-	-	g	ti	main	-	kya	-	ja	-	nu	-	-	-

24. TUM DHUNDHO MUJHE GOPAL

Krishna Bhajan　　　　　　　Singer: Jagjit Singh
Taal: Kaharwa　　　　　　　Chord: DGB$^\flat$　　S=C#
Transpose +1 and play from C scale

tum dhundho mujhe gopal, main khoyi gaiyya teri
sud lo meri gopal, main khoyi gaiyya teri

paanch vikar se hanki jaaye,paanch tatva ki ye dehii
barbas bhatki door kahin main, chain na paaun ab kehi
ye kaisa mayajaal main ulajhi gaiyya teri
sudh lo mori gopal main uljhi gaiyya teri
tum dhoondho mujhe gopal mai, khoyee gaiya teri

jamuna tat na nandan van na gopi gwal koi dikhe
kusum lata na teri chhata na paakhh pakheru koi dikhe
ab sanjh bhayee ghanshyam mai vyakul gaiya teri
sud lo meri gopal main vyakul gaiyya teri
tum dhoondho mujhe gopal mai, khoyee gaiya teri

kit paaun taruvar ki chhaaon jit saje krishna kanhaiya
man ka taap shaap bhatkan ka tum hi haro hari raas rachaiya
ab mook niharun baant prabhu ji main gaiyya teri
sud lo meri gopal, main khoyi gaiyya teri
tum dhundho mujhe gopal, main khoyi gaiyya teri

bansi ke swar naad pe tero madhur taan se mujhe pukaro
radha krishna govind hari har murali manohar naam tiharo
mujhe ubaaro hey gopol main khoyi gaiyya teri
sud lo meri gopal, main khoyi gaiyya teri
tum dhundho mujhe gopal, main khoyi gaiyya teri

Vinod Kumar

TUM DHUNDHO MUJHE GOPAL

dha	ge	n	ti	n	ke	dhi	n	dha	ge	n	ti	n	ke	dhi	n
1	2	3	4	5	6	7	8	1	2	3	4	5	6	7	8

AA   AA   GAB^b B^b B^{b}B^b EE EE EF   GF   EDD
kit paun   truvr ki chhav, jit   saje -- krishna knheya

AA   A AG AB^b B^{b}B^{b}B^b B^b E   E EE   EF GF EDD
mn   ka tap, shap   bhtkn ka, tum hi hro,   hri ras rchaiya

.B^{b}C EE   EEDE   G–FG   E   E DC   D.B^b CD
ab   muk niharun ba--t, prbhu ji main- gaiya teri

GG   A AAG AFG   E   DC D.B^b CD
sudh   lo mori- gopal, mai uljhi gaiya teri

AA   A GA B^{b}B^b B^b B^{b}B^b EE   EE EF   GF   EDD
bnsi ke swar nad pe tero mdhur tan   se   mujhe pukaro

AA   AG   AB^{b}B^b B^{b}B^b B^b EE   EEEF   GF EDD
radha   krishna govind hri   hr, murli   mnohr nam tiharo

.B^b.B^b CEE   E DEG–FG   E   EDC   D.B^b CD
mujhe   ubaro he go-pa--l, main khoii- gaiya   teri

GG   A AAG AFG   E   DC D.B^b CD
sudh   lo mori- gopal, mai   uljhi gaiya teri

Vinod Kumar

25. TUNE MUJHE BULAYA SHERANWALIYE

Film: Asha (1980) Music: Laxmikant Pyarelal
Lyrics: Qaifi Aazmi Singer: Chanchal, Md. Rafi
Taal: Kaharwa Chord: AC'E'   S=C#
Transpose +1 and play from C scale

saanchi jyotawaali maata, teri jai jia kaar
jai jia kaar jai jia kaar jai jia kaar

tune mujhe bulaye sherawaaliye, mein aya mein aya sherawaaliye
oh jyotawaaliye, paharawaaliye, oh mehrawaaliye
tune mujhe bulaye sherawaaliye, mein aya mein aya sherawaaliye

saara jag hai ik banjaara, sab kii manzil tera dwaara
unche parbat lamba rasta, par mein rah na paaya sherawaaliye
tune mujhe bulaye sherawaaliye, mein aya mein aya sherawaaliye

sune mann mein ja gayi baati, tere path mein mil gayi saathi
munh kholun kya tujh se mangu bin mange sab paya sherawaliye
tune mujhe bulaye sherawaaliye, mein aya mein aya sherawaaliye

kaun hai raja kaun bikhari ek barabar tere sare pujari
tune sab ko darshan deke, apne gale lagaya sherawaaliye
tune mujhe bulaye sherawaaliye, mein aya mein aya sherawaaliye

oh prem se bolo jai maata di (jmd), o sare bolo, jmd
o aate bolo, jmd o jate bolo, jmd
o kasht nivare, jmd ma paar utaare, jmd
devi maa bholi, jmd ma bharde jholi, jmd
o jode darpan, jmd maa de ke darshan jmd
jai maata di,

o shrewali ki jai jai, pahada wali ki jai

vaishno rani ki jai, ambe rani ki jai, pahada wali ki jai

TUNE MUJHE BULAYA SHERANWALIYE

dhage	nati	nke	dhin	dhage	nati	nke	dhin	dhage	nati	nke	dhin	dhage	nati	nke	dhin
12	34	56	78	12	34	56	78	12	34	56	78	12	34	56	78

E'E'   E'E'   E'E' E'F$^{#'}$ D'E'F'   E'   E'   E'
saanchi jyoto vali mata,   teri-   jy   jy   kar

D'E'F'   E'   E'   D'E'F' E'   E'   D'E'F'   E'   E'
jy-   jy   kar   jy-   jy   kar   jy-   jy   kar

interlude: flute: E' D' C' B^b D'---- E' C' B^b D'B^b A x2
            piano: G AB^b A A A ---E, G AB^b A A A ---A

AB^{b}C'   B^{b}A   AGA   AA   AAC'B^b
tune-   mujhe bulaya shera valiye-,

  A   B^{b}C'B^b A   GA   B^{b}A   AAA   C'B^{b}A
main aa-ya   main aaya   shera   valiye -2

music: flute: E'D'E'D' C'B^{b}A-

AB^{b}C'   B^{b}A   AGA   AA   AAC'B^b
tune-   mujhe bulaya shera valiye-,

  A   B^{b}C'B^b A   GA   B^{b}A   AAA
main aa-ya   main aaya   shera   valiye

E'   E'E'   D'C'C'D'   D'D'D'   C'BC'   D'   D'C'   AAA-B^b
o   jyotan   valiye-, phada   valiye, o mehra valiye –

Vinod Kumar

AB♭C' B♭A   AGA   AA   AAC'B♭
tune- mujhe bulaya shera valiye-,

A   B♭C'B♭   A   GA   B♭A   AAA
main aa-ya   main aaya shera   valiye -2

interlude: AA C'C' E♭'E♭' E'E' D♭'D♭' D'D' B♭B♭ A-
            GAGB♭ ----- D'C'B♭A------ C'B♭A-

E'-D'C' D'D' D' C'C' B♭AA E'E' D'C'   D'D'   C'B♭A   AA
sa-ra-   jg   hai ik   bnjara, sb   ki- manzil te-ra   dwara

D'D'   D'D'D'D' E'D'F'   E'E'E'---B♭ B♭B♭ B♭B♭B♭B♭ C'B♭ AAA
unche prbt   lmba   rasta ----   unche prbt   lmba rasta

A B♭C'   B♭ A GA   AA   AAC'B♭
pr main-   rh na paya, shera valiye-

AB♭C'   B♭A   AGA   B♭A   AAA
tune-   mujhe bulaya shera valiye....

 A   B♭C' B♭   A   GA   AA   AAC'B♭
main aa-ya main aaya shera   valiye

AB♭C'   B♭A   AGA   B♭A   AAA
tune-   mujhe bulaya   shera valiye....

E'-D'C' D'D' D' C'C' B♭B♭_ AA E'D'C' D'D' D' C'C' B♭B♭   AA
su-ne- mn me jl   gyi bati, tere- pth me mil gaye   sathi

 D'   D'D'   D'C' E'D' F' E'E'---B♭
munh kholun kya tujh se mangu -

B♭   B♭B♭   B♭-D♭′ D♭′C′ B♭   AA
munh kholun   kya-   tujh   se   mangu

A   B♭C′B♭   A GA   AA   AAC′B♭
bin mange- sb paya, shera valiye

AB♭C′   B♭A   AGA   B♭A   AAA   C′B♭A
tune-   mujhe bulaya shera valiye…. o….

A   B♭C′ B♭   A   GA   AA   AAC′B♭
main aa-ya   main aaya shera   valiye

AB♭C′   B♭A   AGA   B♭A   AAA
tune-   mujhe bulaya shera valiye….

E′-D′   C′ D′D′   C′B♭ AAA   E′D′ C′D′D′ D′D′ C′B♭   AAA
kau-n hai raja, kaun bhikhari, ek   brabr tere sare pujari

D′D′   D′D′   D′C′ E′D′F′E′ E′E′---B♭
tune sb   ko- drshn   deke -

B♭B♭   B♭B♭ B♭—D♭′   D♭′C′B♭A AA
tune   sb   ko---   drshn   deke

AAB♭C′ B♭A AGA   AA AAC′B♭
apne-   gle lgaya, shera valiye

AB♭C′   B♭A   AGA   B♭A AAA
tune-   mujhe bulaya shera valiye….

E′ E′E′   D′C′D′   D′D′D′ C′BC′ D′ D′C′   AAA-B♭
o jyotan valiye-, phada valiye, o mehra valiye –

AB♭C′   B♭A   AGA   AA AAC′B♭
tune-   mujhe bulaya shera valiye-,

Vinod Kumar

A   B♭C'B♭   A   GA   B♭A   AAA
main aa-ya   main aaya shera   valiye

C' BC' B♭ AA G AA A   C' BC'B♭ AA G AA A
o prem se bolo, jy mata di   o sa-re bolo, jy mata di

C' BC' BC' G AA A   C' C'B♭ AA G AA A
o aate bolo, jy mata di   o jate bolo, jy mata di

C' BC'   B♭AA G AA A   C' C' B♭AA G AA A
ma ksht   nivare, jy mata di   ma par utare, jy mata di

C'B C' BC' G AA A   C' B♭ AA G AA A
devi ma bholi, jy mata di   bhr de jholi, jy mata di

A GA AA G AA A   A G A AA   G AA A
o jode drpn, jy mata di   ma de ke drshn, jy mata di

 A G AA A G AA A   F'G'A' A'A'   A'G'F'D'-- F'G'A'
o jy mata di, jy mata di   jy--   mata di-----------

A'A'   B♭'B♭' A' B♭'   A'A'C'' B♭' A'G'F'A' A' A'
sheran vali ki jy   pha---da va—li   ki jy

A'A'   B♭'A' A'   B♭'A' A'A' B♭'A' A' B♭'A' A'A'A' B♭'A' A' B♭'A'
vaishno rani ki   jy, ambe rani ki jy, phada vali ki jy

26.   TERE SIWA AB KAUN HAI

Bhajan   Music: Vinod Kumar
Lyrics: Vinod Kumar   Singer: Vinod Kumar
Taal: Rupak   Chord: CE^{b}G   S=C#
Transpose +1 and play from C scale

dukhon ka le ke bojh bhatakun roz subaho shaam
tere siva ab kaun hai duniya mein mere raam

kaisi ye mushkil aa padi har jeev hai pareshaan
insaan jag mein fir rahaa taj chain aur aaraam

dar ka aalam hai ye kaisa tham gaya hai jahaan
is rog ka hal tum bataao ae mere bhagwaan

main das hun tum naath ho kuchh to taras dikhla
bigdi sabhi ban jaaye prabhu aisi karo kirpa

Vinod Kumar

TERE SIWA AB KAUN HAI

ti	ti	na	dhi	na	dhi	na	ti	ti	na	dhi	na	dhi	na
1	2	3	4	5	6	7	1	2	3	4	5	6	7
C′	C′	C′	C′	-	B♭	A♭	B♭	B♭	B♭	B♭	-	A♭	G
A♭	A♭	A♭	A♭	-	G	F	G	-	-	G	A♭	B♭	C′
C′	C′	C′	C′	-	B♭	A♭	B♭	B♭	B♭	B♭	-	A♭	G
A♭	A♭	A♭	A♭	-	G	F	G	-	-	-	-	-	-
G	A♭	G	F	-	E♭	-	F	G	F	E♭	-	D♭	-
E♭	F	E♭	D♭	-	E♭	D♭	C	-	-	D♭	E♭	F	G
G	A♭	G	F	-	E♭	-	F	G	F	E♭	-	D♭	-
E♭	F	E♭	D♭	-	E♭	D♭	C	-	-	-	-	-	-
												C	D♭
												du	-
F	-	F	F	-	E♭	F	G	G	G	G	-	F	G
kho	-	ka	le	-	ke	-	bo	-	jh	bh	t	kun	-
A♭	-	A♭	A♭	A♭	G	A♭	C′	-	-	-	-	E♭′	-
ro	-	j	su	b	ho	-	sha	-	-m	-	-	te	-
D♭′	-	C′	B♭	A♭	C′	-	B♭	-	A♭	G	F	A♭	A♭
re	-	si	va	-	a	b	kau	-	n	hai	-	du	ni
G	-	F	E♭	D♭	E♭	D♭	C	-	-	-	-		
ya	-	me	me	-	re	-	ra	-	-m	-	-		
												C	D♭
												kai	-
F	-	F	F	F	E♭	F	G	-	G	G	-	F	G
si	-	ye	mu	sh	ki	l	aa	-	p	di	-	h	r
A♭	-	A♭	A♭	-	G	A♭	C′	-	-	-	-	E♭′	-
ji	-	v	hai	-	p	re	sha	-	-n	-	-	in	-

$D^{b\prime}$	-	C'	B^b	A^b	C'	-	B^b	-	A^b	G	F	A^b	A^b
sa	-	n	j	g	me	-	fi	r	r	ha	-	t	j
G	-	F	E^b	D^b	E^b	D^b	C	-	-	-	-		
chai	-	n	au	r	aa	-	ra	-	-m	-	-		
												C	D^b
												d	r
F	-	-	F	-	E^b	F	G	-	G	G	-	F	G
ka	-	-	aa	-	l	m	hai	-	ye	kai	-	sa	-
A^b	-	A^b	A^b	-	G	A^b	C'	-	-	-	-	$E^{b\prime}$	-
th	m	g	ya	-	hai	j	ha	-	n	-	-	i	s
$D^{b\prime}$	-	C'	B^b	A^b	C'	-	B^b	-	A^b	G	F	A^b	-
ro	-	g	ka	-	h	l	tu	m	b	ta	-	o	-
G	-	F	E^b	D^b	E^b	D^b	C	-	-	-	-		
ae	-	me	re	-	bh	g	va	-	-n	-	-		
												C	D^b
												main	-
F	-	F	F	-	E^b	F	G	-	G	G	-	F	G
da	-	s	hun	-	tu	m	na	-	th	ho	-	ku	chh
A^b	-	A^b	A^b	-	G	A^b	C'	-	-	-	-	$E^{b\prime}$	$E^{b\prime}$
to	-	t	r	s	di	kh	la	-	-	-	-	bi	g
$D^{b\prime}$	-	C'	B^b	A^b	C'	-	B^b	-	A^b	G	F	A^b	-
di	-	s	bhi	-	b	n	ja	-	ye	pr	bhu	ae	-
G	-	F	E^b	D^b	E^b	D^b	C	-	-	-	-		
si	-	k	ro	-	ki	r	pa	-	-	-	-		

Vinod Kumar

27. UDDHAR KARO BHAGWAN

Hari Bhajan   Singer: Hari Om Sharan
Taal: Kaharwa   Chord: CEG   S=C#
Transpose +1 and play from C scale

siya ram may sab jag jaani karahu pranaam jori jug paani
japahin naam jan aarat bhari mitahin kusankat hohin sukhari
naam let bhav sindhu sukhahi, karahu vichar sujan man maahin

uddhar karo bhagwan tumhari sharan pade
bhav paar karo bhagwan tumhari sharan pade

kaise tera naam dhiyayein kaise tumhari lagan lagaayein
hriday jagaa do gyan tumhari sharan pade

panth maton ki sun sun baatein dwar tere tak panhuch n paate
bhatke beech jahaan tumhari sharan pade

tu hi shyamal krishna murari raam tu hi ganpati tripurari
tum hi bane hanumaan tumhari sharan pade

aesi antar jyot jagaana ham deenon ko sharan lagaana
he prabhu dayaa nidhaan tumhari sharan pade

UDDHAR KARO BHAGWAN

dha	ge	n	ti	n	ke	dhi	n	dha	ge	n	ti	n	ke	dhi	n
1	2	3	4	5	6	7	8	1	2	3	4	5	6	7	8

prelude:

G A B♭ A AC' B♭ A G

E F G- B♭ A G-

EFGA B♭C'B♭ C' B♭C' B♭A- G-

AC' C'B♭ B♭A AG E- FG-

BB BC'C'   B♭A GA FE CDEF EDC

siya ra-m   may sb jg ja--- ni--,

CCD   DDDEF GFE   DC CDEF EDC

krhu prna-m jo-ri jug pa--- ni—

GBB   BC'C' B♭A GAFE CDEF   EDC

jphin na-m jn aa-rt   bha--- ri--,

CCD   DDEFG FED   CCDEF EDC

mitahin kusnkt ho-hin sukha---- ri---

BB BC'C' B♭A GAF   ECDEF EDC

nam le-t   bhv si-ndhu sukha--- hi--,

CCD   DDEF GFE DC CDEF EDC

krhu vicha-r sujn mn ma--- hi--

GGAA   GFE CCCD.B.B CCD   FED CC

uddha-r kro- bhgva---n tumhri shrn pde

 G GAA GFE CCCD.B.B CCD   FED CC

bhv pa-r kro- bhgva--n tumhri shrn pde

Vinod Kumar

FFE   FG-- ABA C'BA GG—GAF-
shrn pde-------- shrn pde-------

FFE   FG-- ABA C'BA GG—
shrn pde-------- shrn pde---

GGAA   GFE CCCD.B.B CCD   FED CC
uddha-r kro- bhgva--n tumhri shrn pde

GGA FED DF   FGG   GGA FEDF   FED ECC
kaise- tera- nam dhiyayen kaise- tumhri- lgn   lgaye

GGC' C'B^{b}A GF FGEC   DDE FED CC
hridy jga- do- gya--n tumhri shrn pde

 G GC'C' C'B^{b}A GFFGEC DDE   FED CC
bhv pa---r kro- bhgva--n tumhri shrn pde

GGAA   GFE CCCD.B.B CCD   FED CC
uddha-r kro- bhgva--n tumhri shrn pde

music: (E D EGF E DEC)x 2 D E G-)

GG   AF ED DD FF GG   GG AF EDF FED   E CC
pnth mton ki- sun sun baten dwar tere tk-   phunch n pate

GC'C'   B^{b}AG FFGEC DDE FED CC
bhtke bii-ch jaha---n tumhri shrn pde

FFE   FG-- ABA   C'BA GG—GAF-
shrn pde-------- shrn pde--------

FFE   FG-- ABA C'BA GG—
shrn pde-------- shrn pde---

G GA F ED   D F   FGG   GG   A F EDFFE   DECC
tu hi- shyaml krishna murari ram tu hi gn-pti   tripurari

GC'   C' C'B♭A   GFFGEC   DDE   FED   CC
tum   hi bne-   hnuma---n tumhri shrn   pde

FFE   FG-- ABA   C'BA GG—GAF-
shrn pde-------- shrn   pde--------

FFE   FG-- ABA   C'BA GG—
shrn pde-------- shrn   pde---

GGAA   GFE CCCD.B.B   CCD   FED CC
uddha-r kro- bhgva--n tumhri shrn pde

GGA FED   DF   FGG   GG GAF EDF   FED ECC
aesi- antr jyoti jgana hm di-no ko--   shrn lgana

GC'   C'C'   B♭AG FFGEC   DDE FED CC
he- prbhu   dya-   nidha---n tumhri shrn pde

FFE   FG-- ABA   C'BA GG—GAF-
shrn pde-------- shrn   pde--------

FFE   FG-- ABA   C'BA GG—
shrn pde-------- shrn   pde---

GGAA   GFE CCCD.B.B CCD   FED CC
uddha-r kro- bhgva--n tumhri shrn pde

Vinod Kumar

28. VRINDAVAN KA KRISHNA KANHAIYA

Film: Miss Meri (1957)   Music: Hemant Kumar
Lyrics: Rajendra Krishna   Singer: Md. Rafi
Taal: Kaharwa   Chord: EGB   S=C#
Transpose +1 and play from C scale
(Krishna Bhajan)

vrindavan ka krishna kanhaiya sabki aankhon ka tara
man hi man kyon jale raadhika mohan to hai sabka pyara

jamuna tat par nand ka lala jab jab raas rachaaye re
tan man dole kaanha aesi bansi madhur bajaaye re
sudh budh bhuli khadi gopiyaan jaane kaisa jaadu dara

rang salona aesa jaise chhayi ho ghat saavan ki
ae ri main to huyi diwaani manmohan manbhawan ki
tere kaaran dekh saanvare chhod diya maine jag saara

VRINDAVAN KA KRISHNA KANHAIYA

dha	-	tin	tin	ta	-	dhin	dhin	dha	-	tin	tin	ta	-	dhin	dhin
1	2	3	4	5	6	7	8	1	2	3	4	5	6	7	8

prelude:

B ---GAG B ---GAG D'---

B A G A ---G A B E' D'   D'—B A G E G –

.B	-	D	-	D	D	D	-	E	E	G	G	G	A	A	-
vrin	-	da	-	v	n	ka	-	kri	sh	n	kn	hai	-	ya	-

G	A	A	G	A	B	B	A	G	-	G	$F^{\#}$	E	-	-	-
s	b	ki	-	aan	-	kho	-	ka	-	ta	-	ra	-	-	-

G	B	B	–	B	A	G	A	B	D'	–	D'	–	D'	D'	–
m	n	hi	–	m	n	kyo	–	j	le	–	ra	–	dhi	ka	–

B	E'	E'	D'	B	–	A	–	G	A	B	A	G	–	E	D
mo	–	h	n	to	–	hai	–	s	b	ka	–	pya	–	ra	

.B	–	D	–	D	D	D	–	E	E	G	G	G	A	A	
vrin	–	da	–	v	n	ka	–	kri	sh	n	kn	hai	–	ya	–

G	A	A	G	A	B	B	A	G	–	G	F$^\#$	E	–	–	–
s	b	ki	–	aan	–	kho	–	ka	–	ta	–	ra	–	–	–

interlude:

D E A – G F$^\#$ E – D E A --G F$^\#$ E–

DEGAB—AGAD'B—

BB AA GG AA BB AA GG A–

GABE'D'—ABBAG GAB—

B	B	B	–	B	A	G	A	B	–	D'	D'	D'	–	D'	–
j	m	na	–	t	t	p	r	nn	–	d	ka	la	–	la	–

D'	E'	E'	D'	E'	F$^{\#\prime}$	F$^{\#\prime}$	E'	D'	–	D'	D$^{b\prime}$	B	–	–	B
j	b	j	b	ra	–	s	r	cha	–	ye	–	re	–	–	–

E'	–	D'	–	E'	–	D'	–	E'	–	D'	D$^{b\prime}$	B	–	–	–
–	–	–	–	–	–	–	–	–	–	–	–	–	–	–	–

B	B	B	–	B	A	G	A	B	–	D'	D'	D'	–	D'	–
j	m	na	–	t	t	p	r	nn	–	d	ka	la	–	la	–

D'	E'	E'	D'	E'	F$^{\#\prime}$	F$^{\#\prime}$	E'	D'	–	D'	D$^{b\prime}$	B	–	–	–
j	b	j	b	ra	–	s	r	cha	–	ye	–	re	–	–	–

E'	–	D'	–	E'	–	D'	–	E'	–	D'	D$^{b\prime}$	B	–	–	–

B	B	B	B	B	A	G	A	B	–	D'	D'	D'	–	D'	–
t	n	m	n	do	–	le	–	kan	–	ha	–	ae	–	si	–

Vinod Kumar

| D' | E' | E' | D' | E' | F#' | F#' | E' | D' | - | D' | D^b' | B | - | - | - |
| bn | - | si | - | m | dhu | r | b | ja | - | ye | - | re | - | - | - |

| A | B | B | D' | D' | - | D' | - | D^b' | D' | - | B | - | B | B | C' |
| su | dh | bu | dh | kho | - | yi | - | kh | di | - | go | - | pi | ya | - |

| A | B | B | C' | B | A | A | G | G | A | B | A | G | F# | E | D |
| ja | - | ne | - | kai | - | sa | - | ja | - | du | - | da | - | ra | - |

interlude:

D E A – G F# E – D E A -- G F# E–

DEGAB—AGAD'B—

BB AA GG AA BB AA GG A-

GABE'D'—ABBAG GAB--

BB   BBAGA BD'D'   D'D' D'E'E'D' E'F#' F#'E' D' D'D^b'   B
rng slo -na -ae -sa jaise chha -ii - ho   ght savn   ki

music: B E'- D'- E'- D'- E'- D'– D^b' B

BB   BA GA   BD'   D'D'D' D'E'E'D'E'F#' F#'E' D' -D'D^b' B
aeri skhi main - huii divani mnmohn   mnbhavn   ki

ABBD' D'D'D' D'D' D^b'BBC'
te -re - karn   dekh san -vre -

AB   C'BA   A–GA   BA   GF#E
chhod diya main -ne - jg   sara

29. WAHAAN KAUN HAI TERA

Film: Guide (1965)
Lyrics: Shailendra
Taal: Daadra
Transpose +2 and play from C scale

Music: Sachindev Burman
Singer: Sachindev Burman
Chord: DFA S=D

wahaan kaun hai tera musafir, jaayega kahaan
dam le le ghadi bhar, ye chhaiyaan, paayega kahaan

beet gaye din, pyar ke pal-chhin, sapna bani ye raatein
bhul gaye vo, tu bhi bhula de, <u>pyar ki vo mulaqatein</u> -2
sab dur andera, musafir, jaayega kahaan

koi bhi teri, rah na dikhe, nain bichhaye na koi
dard se tere, koi na tadpa, <u>aankh kisi ki na royi</u>-2
kahe kisko tu mera, musafir, jaayega kahaan

kahte hain gyani, duniya hai paani, paani pe likhi likhaayi
hai sabki dekhi, hai sabki jaani, <u>haath kisi ke na aayi</u>-2
kuchh tera na mera, musafir, jaayega kahaan

Vinod Kumar

WAHAAN KAUN HAI TERA

dha	dhi	na	dha	tu	na	dha	dhi	na	dha	tu	na
1	2	3	4	5	6	1	2	3	4	5	6
music: FFF, FFF, FFF, F											
										F	F
										v	ha
A	-	A	A	G	-	-	-	A	A	G	-
kau	-n	hai	te	ra	-	-	-	mu	sa	fi	-r
-	-	A	A	G	F	F	-	D	-	F	F
-	-	ja	ye	ga	k	ha	-	-	-	d	m
A	A	A	A	G	-	-	-	A	A	G	-
le	le	gh	di	bh	r	-	-	ye	chhii	yan	-
B^b	-	B^b	A	G	F	F	-	D	-	F	F
-	-	pa	ye	ga	k	ha	-	-	-	v	ha
A	-	A	A	G	-	-	-	A	A	G	-
kau	-n	hai	te	ra	-	-	-	mu	sa	fi	-r
-	-	A	A	G	F	F	-	D	-	F	F
-	-	ja	ye	ga	k	ha	-	-	-	v	ha
A	-	A	A	G	-	GA	B^b	A	G	F	-
kau	-n	hai	te	ra	-	-	-	-	-	-	-
music: FGF FC' FAGFFD, FGF FC' FAGF-											
flute: D' ------ C' ---- C' ---- B^b ------ A G F –											
FGF FC' FAGFFD, FGF FC' FAGF-											
flute: C' ---- B^b GF A A^b A											
A	-B^b	B^b	C'	A	-	A	C'	F	B^b	A	-
bii	-t	g	ye	din	-	-	-	-	-	-	-

A	B♭	C'	B♭	A	-	A	C'	A	F	D	-
pya	-r	ke	pl	chhin	-	-	-	-	-	-	-
D'	D'	D'	D'	C'D'	-	B	-	C'	-	-	-
sp	na	b	ni	ye-	-	ra	-	ten	-	-	-
-	B	C'D'	B♭	A	-						
-	-	-	-	-	-						
A	B♭	C'	B♭	A	-	A	C'	F	B♭	A	-
bhu	l	g	ye	vo	-	-	-	-	-	-	-
A	B♭	C'	B♭	A	-	A	C'	A	F	D	-
tu	bhi	bhu	la	de	-	-	-	-	-	-	-
D'	-	D'	D'	C'	D'	B	-	C'	-	C'D'	F'
pya	-r	ki	vo	mu	la	ka	-	ten	-	-	-
F'	-	E♭'	D'	C'	B♭	A	-	G	-	F	F
pya	-r	ki	vo	mu	la	ka	-	ten	-	s	b
F	G	B♭	A	G	-	-	-	-	-	F	F
du	-r	an	dhe	ra	-	-	-	-	-	s	b
F	G	B♭	A	G	-	-	-	A	A	G	-
du	-r	an	dhe	ra	-	-	-	mu	sa	fi	-r
-	-	A	A	G	F	F	-	D	D	F	F
-	-	ja	ye	ga	k	ha	-	-	-	d	m
A	A	-	-	F	F	B♭	B♭	-	A	F	F
le	le	-	-	d	m	le	le	-	-	d	m
A	A	A	A	G	-	-	-	A	A	G	-
le	le	gh	di	bhr	-	-	-	ye	chhii	yan	-

B^b	-	B^b	A	G	F	F	-	D	D	F	F
-	-	pa	ye	ga	k	ha	-	-	-	v	ha

A	-	A	A	G	-	GA	B^b	A	G	F	-
kau	-n	hai	te	ra	-	-	-	-	-	-	-

C' ----------- $E^{b'}$ D' C' B^b
ho -------------------------

A A A B^b C' B^b C' D' B^b– A –
mu sa fi ---------------- r

D' D' D' C' D' F' D' C' B^b A$B^b$$C'$ –
tu jayega kahan ------------

30. YE KAUN CHITRAKAR HAI

Film: Boond jo ban gayi moti (1967)   Music: Satish Bhatia
Lyrics: Bharat Vyas   Singer: Mukesh
Taal: Daadra   Chord: DFA S=C#
Transpose +1 and play from C scale

hari bhari vasundhara pe neela neela ye gagan

ke jis pe baadlon ki paalki uda raha pawan

dishayein dekho rang bhari,

dishayein dekho rang bhari, chamak rahi umang bhari

ye kisne phul phul pe

ye kisne phul phul pe, kiya singar hai

ye kaun chitrakar hai, ye kaun chitrakar

ye kaun chitrakar hai

tapasviyon si hain atal ye parvaton ki chotiyaan

ye barf ki ghumerdaar ghaatiyaan

dhwaja se ye khade hue

dhwaja se ye khade hue hain vriksh devdaar ke
galeeche ye gulab ke bageeche ye bahaar ke
ye kis kavi ki kalpana,
ye kis kavi ki kalpana, ka chamatkar hai,
ye kaun chitrakar hai, ye kaun chitrakar
ye kaun chitrakar hai

kudrat ki is pavitrata ko tum nihaar lo, ha ha ha
iske gunon ko apne man mein tum utaar lo, ha ha ha
chamka lo aaj laalima,
chamka lo aaj laalima apne lalaat
kan kan se jhaankti tumhein chhavi viraat ki
apni to aankh ek hai,
apni to aankh ek hai, uski hazaar hai
ye kaun chitrakar hai, ye kaun chitrakar
ye kaun chitrakar hai

YE KAUN CHITRAKAR HAI

dha	dhi	na	dha	tu	na	dha	dhi	na	dha	tu	na
1	2	3	4	5	6	1	2	3	4	5	6
											D
											h
D	-	D	D	-	D	D	-	D	D	-	D
ri	-	h	ri	-	v	sun	-	dh	ra	-	pe
C	-	C	C	-	C	F	-	E^b	D	-	-
ni	-	la	ni	-	la	ye	-	g	gn	-	-
.A	-	-	C	-	-	F	-	E^b	D	-	D
-	-	-	-	-	-	-	-	-	-	-	ye

D	D	D	D	-	D	D	-	D	D	-	D
ji	s	pe	ba	-	d	lon	-	ki	pa	-	l
C	-	C	C	-	C	F	-	E♭	D	-	-
ki	-	u	da	-	r	ha	-	p	vn	-	-
.A	-	-	C	-	-	F	-	E♭	D	-	D
-	-	-	-	-	-	-	-	-	-	-	di
D	-	D	F	-	F	G	G	A♭	G	-	-
sha	-	yen	de	-	kho	rn	g	bh	ri	-	-
-	-	-	-	-	-	-	-	-	A♭	F	D
-	-	-	-	-	-	-	-	-	-	-	di
D	-	D	F	-	F	G	G	A♭	G	-	F
sha	-	yen	de	-	kho	rn	g	bh	ri	-	ch
D	D	D	F	-	F	G	G	A♭	G	-	G
m	k	r	hi	-	u	man	g	bh	ri	-	ye
A	A	A	C′	-	C′	D′	-	E♭′	D′	-	-
ki	s	ne	fu	-	l	fu	-	l	pe	-	-
-	-	-	-	-	-	-	-	-	C′	A	A
-	-	-	-	-	-	-	-	-	-	-	ye
A	A	A	A	-	D′	B♭	-	B♭	A	-	G
ki	s	ne	fu	-	l	fu	-	l	pe	-	ki
F	-	F	F	-	E	F	-	-	-	-	D
ya	-	sin	ga	-	r	hai	-	-	-	-	ye
D	-	D	E♭	-	F	E♭	-	D	D	-	.B♭
kau	-	n	chi	-	tr	ka	-	r	hai	-	ye

D	-	D	E♭	-	D	D	-	-	-	-	D
kau	-	n	chi	-	tr	ka	-	r	-	-	ye
A	-	-	-	-	-	-	-	-	A	C'	-
kau	-	-	-	-	-	-	-	-	-	-	n
A	-	G	F	-	E	F	-	-	-	-	.B♭
chi	-	tr	ka	-	r	hai	-	-	-	-	ye
D	-	D	E♭	-	F	E♭	-	D	D	-	.B♭
kau	-	n	chi	-	tr	ka	-	r	hai	-	ye
D	-	D	E♭	-	D	D	-	-	-	-	-
kau	-	n	chi	-	tr	ka	-	r	-	-	-

interlude:

A	A	-	B♭	A	-	C'	C'	-	C'	C'	-
A	A	-	B♭	A	-	G	-	-	-	-	-
F	F	-	G	A	-	E♭	E♭	-	F	G	-
F#	F#	-	F	F	-	E♭	E♭	-	D	-	-

mauth organ: D-E♭ F---- GA— D-E♭ F-E♭ F-E♭ D---

											A
											t
A	A	A	A	-	B♭	G	-	G	G	-	A
p	s	vi	yon	-	si	hain	-	a	tl	-	ye
F	-	F	F	-	F	C'	-	B♭	A	-	A
p	r	b	ton	-	ki	cho	-	ti	ya	-	ye
A	A	A	A	-	B♭	G	-	G	G	-	G
b	r	f	ki	-	ghu	me	-	r	da	-	r
A	-	F	F	-	F	C'	-	B♭	A	-	A
ghe	-	r	da	-	r	gha	-	ti	ya	-	dhw

126

A	-	A	C′	-	C′	D′	-	E^{b}′	D′	-	-
ja	-	se	ye	-	kh	de	-	hu	e	-	-
-	-	-	-	-	-	-	-	-	C′	A	C′
-	-	-	-	-	-	-	-	-	-	-	dhw
F	-	F	A	-	B	C′	-	D′	C′	-	C′
ja	-	se	ye	-	kh	de	-	hu	e	-	hain
B	-	B	G	-	G	B^{b}	-	B^{b}	A	-	A
vri	-	ksh	de	-	v	da	-	r	ke	-	g
C′	-	C′	C′	-	B^{b}	A	-	A	A	-	A
li	-	che	ye	-	gu	la	-	b	ke	-	b
C′	-	C′	C′	-	B^{b}	A	-	A	A	-	A
gi	-	che	ye	-	b	ha	-	r	ke	-	ye
A	A	A	C′	-	C′	D′	-	E^{b}′	D′	-	-
ki	s	k	vi	-	ki	k	l	p	na	-	
-	-	-	-	-	-	-	-	-	C′	A	A
-	-	-	-	-	-	-	-	-	-	-	ye
A	-	A	A	-	D′	B^{b}	-	A	G	-	G
ki	s	k	vi	-	ki	k	l	p	na	-	ka
F	F	F	F	-	E	F	-	-	-	-	D
ch	m	t	ka	-	r	hai	-	-	-	-	ye
D	-	D	E^{b}	-	F	E^{b}	-	D	D	-	.B^{b}
kau	-	n	chi	-	tr	ka	-	r	hai	-	ye
D	-	D	E^{b}	-	D	D	-	-	-	-	
kau	-	n	chi	-	tr	ka	-	r	-	-	

31. SARGAM OR ALANKAR OR PALTE

S R G M P D N S'
S' N D P M G R S

SS RR GG MM PP DD NN S'S'
S'S' NN DD PP MM GG RR SS

SSS RRR GGG MMM PPP DDD NNN S'S'S'
S'S'S' NNN DDD PPP MMM GGG RRR SSS

SR RG GM MP PD DN NS'
S'N ND DP PM MG GR RS

SRG- RGM- GMP- MPD PDN- DNS'-
S'ND- NDP- DPM- PMG- MGR- GRS-

SRGM RGMP GMPD MPDN PDNS'
S'NDP NDPM DPMG PMGR MGRS

SRGMP RGMPD GMPDN MPDNS'
S'NDPM NDPMG DPMGR PMGRS

SG RM GP MD PN DS'
S'D NP DM PG MR GS

SM RP GD MN PS'
S'P NM DG PR MS

SP RD GN MS'
S'M NG DR PS

Vinod Kumar

SD RN GS'
S'G NR DS

SRSRG– RGRGM– GMGMP- MPMPD– PDPDN– DNDNS'-
S'NS'ND- NDNDP– DPDPM– PMPMG–MGMGR– GRGRS-

SRGSRSRG RGMRGRGM GMPGMGMP
MPDMPMP PDNPDPD DNS'DNDNS'

S'NDS'NS'ND NDPNDNDP DPMDPDPM
PMGPMPMG MGMGMGR GRSGRGRS

S
SRS
SRGRS
SRGMGRS
SRGMPMGRS
SRGMPDPMGRS
SRGMPDNDPMGRS
SRGMPDNS'S'NDPMGRS

S'
S'N S'
S'N D N S'
S'N D P D N S'
S'N D P M P D N S'
S'N D P M G M P D N S'
S'N D P M G R G M P D N S'
S'N D P M G R S R G M P D N S'

S-SRG- R-RGM- G-GMP- M-MPD- P-PDN- D-DNS'-
S'-S'ND- N-NDP- D-DPM- P-PMG- M-MGR- G-GRS-

RS GR MG PM DP ND S'N R'S'
NS' DN PD MP GM RG SR .NS

SGR RMG GPM MDP PND DS'N NR'S'
S'DN NPD DMP PGM MRG GSR R.NS

.P P .DD .NN SS' RR' GG' MM'
M'M G'G R'R S'S N.N D.D P.P

S R̲ G̲ M P D̲ N̲ S'
S' N̲ D̲ P M G̲ R̲ S

S R̲ G M P D̲ N S'
S' N D̲ P M G R̲ S

32. Other books of Vinod Kumar

Mukesh Songs' Western Notes, Part-1, 2

Lata Songs' Western Notes

Kishore Songs' Western Notes, Part-1, 2

Md. Rafi Songs' Western Notes, Part-1,2,3,4

Asha Songs' Western Notes

SD Burman and Yesudas Songs' Western Notes

Manna Dey Songs' Western Notes

Kumar Shanu Songs' Western Notes

Mahendra Kapoor Songs' Western Notes

Composer SD Burman Songs' Western Notes

Suman Kalyanpur Songs' Western Notes

51 Superhit Gazals' Western Notes sargam

Bhajan Western Notes, Part-1,2,3,4

Sloan Duployan Shorthand book

Sabad and Punjabi Songs' Western Notes

These Books are also available in English SRGM and Western CDEFG style at notionpress.com and amazon.in and at Flipkart.com

For English SRGM books search... (Singer name) 51 Songs' Sargam, book.

For Western CDEFG books search... (Singer name) Songs' Western Notes, book.

If you like the books, pl. tell others.

vinod kumar (vinod66vk@gmail.com)

Vinod Kumar

Scan below QR Code from your mobile to get Vinod Kumar's (Singer name) 51 Songs' Sargam books from Flipkart.com site . (Hindi, English, Western all)

Scan below QR Code from your mobile to get Vinod Kumar's (Singer name) 51 Songs' Sargam books from Amazon.in site . (Hindi, English, Western all)

ASHA
SONGS' WESTERN NOTES
Love Songs
Sad Songs
ASHA Songs Lyrics in English & Notations in CDEFG
CDEFGABC'
VINOD KUMAR
LATA
SONGS WESTERN NOTES
Love Songs
Sad Songs
LATA SONGS LYRICS AND WESTERN NOTES
CDEFGABC'
VINOD KUMAR
SUPERHIT 51
GAZALS'
WESTERN NOTES
Gazals and Nazams in English and Western Notes
CDEFGABC'
VINOD KUMAR
Composer
S.D. Burman
Songs' Western Notes Part-1
CDEFGABC
VINOD KUMAR
KISHORE
SONGS' WESTERN NOTES
Part-2
CDEFGABC'
VINOD KUMAR
KISHORE
SONGS' WESTERN NOTES
CDEFGABC
VINOD KUMAR
KUMAR SHANU
SONGS' WESTERN NOTES
TU MERI ZINDAGI HAI
Songs Lyrics in English and Notations in CDEF
CDEFGABC'
VINOD KUMAR
MANNA DEY
Songs' Western Notes
CDEFGABC'
MD RAFI
SONGS' WESTERN NOTES Part-4
Mujhe ishq hai tujhi se....
Songs' Lyrics in English and Notations in CDEF
CDEFGABC'
VINOD KUMAR
Md RAFI
SONGS' WESTERN NOTES Part-3
Songs' Lyrics in English and Notations in CDEF
CDEFGABC'
VINOD KUMAR
Part-2
Chal ud ja re panchhi
ke ab ye desh hua begana
CDEFGABC'
VINOD KUMAR
Md RAFI
SONGS' WESTERN NOTES
Songs' Lyrics in English and Notations in CDEF
CDEFGABC'
VINOD KUMAR
S.D. BURMAN
SONGS' WESTERN NOTES
Bole to parsun kahin bati sunal de
Songs' Lyrics in English and Notations in CDEF
CDEFGABC
VINOD KUMAR
MUKESH
SONGS' WESTERN NOTES Part-2
CDEFGABC
VINOD KUMAR
MUKESH
SONGS' WESTERN NOTES
Sad Songs
Love Songs
Songs Lyrics in English and Notations in CDEF
CDEFGABC'
VINOD KUMAR
Hindi सा रे ग म
English SRGM
And
Western CDEF
All type books

Vinod Kumar

www.ingramcontent.com/pod-product-compliance
Lightning Source LLC
Chambersburg PA
CBHW071330140726
47996CB00005B/1902